I CALL IT HERESY!

I Call It Heresy!

A.W. Tozer

Compiled and edited by
Gerald B. Smith

CHRISTIAN PUBLICATIONS
CAMP HILL, PENNSYLVANIA

Christian Publications
3825 Hartzdale Drive, Camp Hill, PA 17011
www.cpi-horizon.com

Faithful, biblical publishing since 1883

ISBN: 0-87509-459-7
LOC Catalog Card Number: 91-72300
© 1991 by Christian Publications
All rights reserved
Printed in the United States of America

98 99 00 01 02   7 6 5 4 3

CONTENTS

I Call It Heresy!

As obedient children, do not conform to
the evil desires you had when you lived in
ignorance. (1 Peter 1:14)

The Scriptures do not teach that the Person of Jesus Christ nor any of the important offices which God has given Him can be divided or ignored according to the whims of men.

Therefore, I must be frank in my feeling that a notable heresy has come into being throughout our evangelical Christian circles—the widely accepted concept that we humans can choose to accept Christ only because we need Him as Savior and we have the right to postpone our obedience to Him as Lord as long as we want to!

This concept has sprung naturally from a misunderstanding of what the Bible actually says about Christian discipleship and obedience. It is now found in nearly all of our full gospel literature. I confess that I was among those who preached it before I began to pray earnestly, to study diligently and meditate with anguish over the whole matter.

I think the following is a fair statement of what I was taught in my early Christian experience and it certainly needs a lot of modifying and a great many qualifiers to save us from being in error.

"We are saved by accepting Christ as our Savior; we are sanctified by accepting Christ as our Lord; we may do the first without doing the second!"

The truth is that salvation apart from obedience is unknown in the sacred Scriptures. Peter makes it plain that we are "chosen according to the foreknowledge of God the Father, through the sanctifying work of the Spirit for obedience" (1 Peter 1:2).

What a tragedy that in our day we often hear the gospel appeal made on this kind of basis:

"Come to Jesus! You do not have to obey anyone. You do not have to change anything. You do not have to give up anything, alter anything, surrender anything, give back anything—just come to Him and believe in Him as Savior!"

So they come and believe in the Savior. Later on, in a meeting or conference, they will hear another appeal:

"Now that you have received Him as Savior, how would you like to take Him as Lord?"

The fact that we hear this everywhere does

not make it right. To urge men and women to believe in a divided Christ is bad teaching for no one can receive half of Christ, or a third of Christ, or a quarter of the Person of Christ! We are not saved by believing in an office nor in a work.

I heard well-meaning workers say, "Come and believe on the finished work." That work will not save you. The Bible does not tell us to believe in an office or a work, but to believe on the Lord Jesus Christ Himself, the Person who has done that work and holds those offices.

Now, note again, Peter's emphasis on obedience among the scattered and persecuted Christians of his day.

It seems most important to me that Peter speaks of his fellow Christians as "obedient children." He was not giving them a command or exhortation to be obedient. In effect, he said, "Assuming that you are believers, I therefore gather that you are also obedient. So now, as obedient children, do so and so."

Obedience taught throughout Bible

Brethren, I would point out that obedience is taught throughout the entire Bible and that true obedience is one of the toughest requirements of the Christian life. Apart from obedience, there can be no salvation, for salvation without obedience is a self-contradictory impossibility. The essence of sin is rebellion against divine authority.

God said to Adam and Eve, "You must not eat from the tree of the knowledge of good and evil, for when you eat of it you will surely die" (Genesis 2:17). Here was a divine requirement calling for obedience on the part of those who had the power of choice and will.

In spite of the strong prohibition, Adam and Eve stretched forth their hands and tasted of the fruit and thus they disobeyed and rebelled, bringing sin upon themselves.

Paul writes very plainly and directly in the book of Romans about "one man's dis-obedience"—and this is a stern word by the Holy Spirit through the apostle—by one man's disobedience came the downfall of the human race!

In John's Gospel, the Word is very plain and clear that sin is lawlessness, that sin is dis-obedience to the law of God. Paul's picture of sinners in Ephesians concludes that "the people of the world are the children of disobedience." Paul certainly means that disobedience charac-terizes them, conditions them, molds them. Disobedience has become a part of their nature.

All of this provides background for the great, continuing question before the human race: "Who is boss?" This breaks down into a series of three questions: "To whom do I belong?" "To whom do I owe allegiance?" and "Who has authority to require obedience of me?"

Now, I suppose of all the people in the world Americans have the most difficult time in giving obedience to anyone or anything. Americans are supposed to be sons of freedom. We ourselves were the outcropping of a revolt. We spawned a revolution, pouring the tea overboard in the Boston harbor. We made speeches and said, "That sound of the clash of arms is carried on every wind that blows from the Boston Commons" and finally, "Give me liberty or give me death!"

That is in the American blood and when anyone says, "You owe obedience," we immediately bristle! In the natural sense, we do not take kindly to the prospect of yielding obedience to anyone.

In the same sense, the people of this world have a quick and ready answer to the questions: "To whom do I belong?" and "To whom do I owe obedience?"

Their answer is: "I belong to myself. No one has authority to require my obedience!"

In the name of "individualism"

Our generation makes a great deal out of this, and we give it the name of "individualism." On the basis of our individuality we claim the right of self-determination.

In an airplane, the pilot who sits at the controls determines where that plane is going. He must determine the destination.

Now, if God had made us humans to be mere machines we would not have the power of self-determination. But since He made us in His own image and made us to be moral creatures, He has given us that power of self-determination.

I would insist that we do not have the right of self-determination because God has given us only the power to choose evil. Seeing that God is a holy God and we are moral creatures having the power but not the right to choose evil, no man has any right to lie.

We have the power to lie but no man has any right to lie.

We have the power to steal—I could go out and get myself a better coat than the one I own. I could slip out through a side door and get away with the coat. I have that power but I do not have the right!

I have the power to use a knife, a razor or a gun to kill another person—but I do not have that right! I have only the power to do it.

Actually, we only have the right to be good— we never have the right to be bad because God is good. We only have the right to be holy; we never have the right to be unholy. If you are unholy you are using a right that is not yours. Adam and Eve had no moral right to eat of that tree of good and evil, but they took it and usurped the right that was not theirs.

The poet Tennyson must have thought about this for he wrote in his *In Memoriam:* "Our wills are ours, we know not how; our wills are ours to make them Thine!"

Oh, this mystery of a man's free will is far too

great for us! Tennyson said, "We know not how." But then he girds himself and continues, "Yes, our wills are ours to make them Thine." And that is the only right we have here to make our wills the wills of God, to make the will of God our will!

God is the Sovereign

We must remember that God is Who He is and we are what we are. God is the Sovereign and we are the creatures. He is the Creator and therefore He has a right to command us with the obligation that we should obey. It is a happy obligation, I might say, for "His yoke is easy and His burden is light."

Now, this is where I raise the point again of our human insistence that Christ may sustain a divided relationship toward us. This is now so commonly preached that to oppose it or object to it means that you are sticking your neck out and you had best be prepared for what comes.

But how can we insist and teach that our Lord Jesus Christ can be our Savior without being our Lord? How can we continue to teach that we can be saved without any thought of obedience to our Sovereign Lord?

I am satisfied that when man believes on Jesus Christ he must believe on the whole Lord Jesus Christ—not making any reservation! I am satisfied that it is wrong to look upon Jesus as a kind of divine nurse to whom we can go when sin has made us sick, and after He has helped us, to say "Goodbye"—and go on our own way.

Suppose I slip into a hospital and tell the staff I need a blood transfusion or perhaps an X-ray of my gall bladder. After they have ministered to me and given their services, do I just slip out of the hospital again with a cheery "Goodbye"—as though I owe them nothing and it was kind of them to help me in my time of need?

That may sound like a grotesque concept to you, but it does pretty well draw the picture of those who have been taught that they can use Jesus as a Savior in their time of need without owning Him as Sovereign and Lord and without owing Him obedience and allegiance.

No such concept of salvation

The Bible never in any way gives us such a concept of salvation. Nowhere are we ever led to believe that we can use Jesus as a Savior and not own Him as our Lord. He is the Lord and as the Lord He saves us, because He has all of the offices of Savior and Christ and High Priest and Wisdom and Righteousness and Sanctification and Redemption! He is all of these things and all of these are embodied in Him as Christ the Lord.

My brethren, we are not allowed to come to Jesus Christ as shrewd, clever operators saying, "We will take this and this, but we won't take that!" We do not come to Him as one who, buying furniture for his house, declares: "I will take this table but I don't want that chair"—dividing it up!

No, sir! It is either all of Christ or none of Christ!

I believe we need to preach again a whole Christ to the world—a Christ who does not need our apologies, a Christ who will not be divided, a Christ who will either be Lord of all or who will not be Lord at all!

I think it is important to agree that true salvation restores the right of a Creator-creature relationship because it acknowledges God's right to our fellowship and communion.

You see, in our time we have over-emphasized the psychology of the sinner's condition. We spend much time describing the woe of the sinner, the grief of the sinner and the great burden he carries. He does have all of these, but we have over-emphasized them until we forget the principal fact—that the sinner is actually a rebel against properly constituted authority!

That is what makes sin, sin. We are rebels. We are sons of disobedience. Sin is the breaking of the law and we are in rebellion and we are fugitives from the just laws of God while we are sinners.

By way of illustration, suppose a man escapes from prison. Certainly he will have grief. He is going to be in pain after bumping logs and stones and fences as he crawls and hides away in the dark. He is going to be hungry and cold and weary. His beard will grow long and he will be tired and cramped and cold—all of these will happen, but they are incidental to the fact that he is a fugitive from justice and a rebel against law.

So it is with sinners. Certainly they are heartbroken and they carry a heavy load. The Bible takes full account of these things; but they are incidental to the fact that the reason the sinner is what he is, is because he has rebelled against the laws of God and he is a fugitive from divine judgement.

It is that which constitutes the nature of sin; not the fact that he carries a heavy load of misery and sadness and guilt. These things constitute only the outcropping of the sinful nature, but the root of sin is rebellion against God. Does not the sinner say: "I belong to myself—I owe allegiance to no one unless I choose to give it!" That is the essence of sin.

But thankfully, salvation reverses that and restores the former relationship so that the first thing the returning sinner does is to confess: "Father, I have sinned against heaven and against you. I am no longer worthy to be called your son; make me like one of your hired men" (Luke 15:18–19).

Thus, in repentance, we reverse that relationship and we fully submit to the Word of God and the will of God, as obedient children.

Now that happiness of all the moral creatures

lies right here, brethren, in the giving of obedience to God. The Psalmist cried out in Psalm 103:21, "Praise the Lord, all his heavenly hosts,/ you his servants who do his will."

The angels in heaven find their complete freedom and highest happiness in obeying the commandments of God. They do not find it a tyranny—they find it a delight.

I have been looking again into the mysteries in the first chapter of Ezekiel and I don't understand it. There are creatures with four faces and four wings, strange beings doing strange things. They have wheels and still other wheels in the middle of the wheels. There is fire coming out of the north and there are creatures going straight ahead and some that lower their wings and wave them. Strange, beautiful beings and they are all having the time of their lives utterly, completely delighted with the Presence of God and that they could serve God!

A world of disobedience

On the other hand, hell is certainly the world of disobedience. Everything else that may be said about hell may be true, but this one thing is the essence—hell is the world of the rebel! Hell is the Alcatraz for the unconstituted rebels who refuse to surrender to the will of God.

I thank God that heaven is the world of God's obedient children. Whatever else we may say of its pearly gates, its golden streets and its jasper walls, heaven is heaven because children of the Most High God find they are in their normal sphere as obedient moral beings.

Jesus said there are fire and worms in hell, but that is not the reason it is hell. You might endure worms and fire, but for a moral creature to know and realize that he is where he is because he a rebel—that is the essence of hell and judgment. It is the eternal world of all the disobedient rebels who have said, "I owe God nothing!"

This is the time given us to decide. Each person makes his own decision as to the eternal world he is going to inhabit.

A *serious decision*

This is a serious matter of decision. You do not come to this decision as though it were a matter of being interviewed for a job or getting your diploma at a school.

We have no basis to believe that we can come casually and sprightly to the Lord Jesus and say, "I have come for some help, Lord Jesus. I understand that you are the Savior so I am going to believe and be saved and then I am going to turn away and think about the other matters of lordship and allegiance and obedience at some time in the future."

I warn you—you will not get help from Him in that way for the Lord will not save those whom He cannot command!

He will not divide His offices. You cannot

believe on a half-Christ. We take Him for what He is—the anointed Savior and Lord who is King of kings and Lord of lords! He would not be who He is if He saved us and called us and chose us without the understanding that He can also guide and control our lives.

Brethren, I believe in the deeper Christian life and experience—oh yes! But I believe we are mistaken when we try to add the deeper life to an imperfect salvation, obtained imperfectly by an imperfect concept of the whole thing.

Under the working of the Spirit of God through such men as Finney and Wesley, no one would ever dare to rise in a meeting and say, "I am a Christian" if he had not surrendered his whole being to God and had taken Jesus Christ as his Lord. It was only then that he could say, "I am saved!"

Today, we let them say they are saved no matter how imperfect and incomplete the transaction, with the proviso that the deeper Christian life can be tacked on at some time in the future.

Can it be that we really think that we do not owe Jesus Christ our obedience?

We have owed Him obedience ever since the second we cried out to Him for salvation, and if we do not give Him that obedience, I have reason to wonder if we are really converted!

I see things and I hear of things that Christian people are doing. As I watch them operate within the profession of Christianity I do raise the question of whether they have been truly converted.

Brethren, I believe it is the result of faulty teaching to begin with. They thought of the Lord as a hospital and Jesus as chief of staff to fix up poor sinners that had gotten into trouble!

"Fix me up, Lord," they have insisted, "so that I can go on my own way!"

That is bad teaching, brethren. It is filled with self-deception. Let us look unto Jesus our Lord, high, holy, wearing the crowns, Lord of lords and King of all, having a perfect right to command full obedience from all of His saved people!

Remember what the Bible says

Just remember what the Bible says about the Person and the titles and the offices of Jesus.

"God has made this Jesus whom you crucified both Lord and Christ" (Acts 2:36b). Jesus means Savior, Lord means Sovereign, Christ means Anointed One. The apostle, therefore, did not preach Jesus as Savior—he preached to them Jesus as Lord and Christ and Savior, never dividing His person or offices.

Remember, too, that Paul wrote to the Roman Christians:

> But what does it say? "The word is near you; it is in your mouth and in your heart," that is, the word of faith we are proclaiming: That if you confess with your

mouth, "Jesus is Lord," and believe in your heart that God raised him from the dead, you will be saved. (10:8–9)

The apostle did not say that "You shall confess with your mouth the Savior." He said,

For it is with your heart that you believe and are justified, and it is with your mouth that you confess and are saved . . . For there is no difference between Jew and Gentile—the same Lord is Lord of all who call on him, for everyone who calls on the name of the Lord will be saved. (verses 10, 12–13)

Three times he calls Jesus Lord in these passages telling us how to be saved. He says that faith in the Lord Jesus plus confession of that faith to the world brings salvation to us!

God desires that we be honest with Him above everything else. Search the Scriptures, read the New Testament, and if you see that I have given a germ of truth, then I urge you to do something about it. If you have been led to believe imperfectly in a divided Savior, be glad that there is still time for you to do something about it!

The Bible Is
Not Dead!

*For you have been born again . . . through
the living and enduring word of God . . .
And this is the word that was preached
to you.* (1 Peter 1:23, 25)

There are Christians among us today who
seem to feel that their spiritual lives
would have been greatly helped if they could
have had voice-to-voice and person-to-person
counsel from our Lord or from the Apostle
Peter or Paul.

I know it is fair to say that if one of the
apostles or any of the great early fathers of the
church could return to this world from their
yesteryear, there would not be room to contain
the crowds that would rush in.

If it were that St. Augustus or Chrysostom or
Francis of Assisi or Knox or Luther or any of
the greats who have lived were to be present to
speak, we would all give our closest attention

and listen as though we were hearing indeed a very word from God.

Under the circumstances, we cannot hope to hear from men of God who centuries ago completed their ministries and went to be with the Lord. The voices of the great saints and mighty warriors of yesterday can no longer be heard in this 20th century.

However, there is good news for those who are anxious to hear a word from the Lord! If we have a mind to listen, we may still "hear" the voice of an apostle for we are dealing with the words written by the man, Peter. He was indeed a great saint, even though we may not consider him the greatest of the apostles. I think it is safe to say that he was the second of the apostles, Paul alone, perhaps, having a higher place than the man, Peter.

So, as we look into his message, Peter will be speaking to us, even though it is through an "interpreter."

Often our missionaries have told us of difficult times they have had with interpreters. The expression of the missionary may go in one way and come out with a different sense to the hearer, and I think when we expound the Scriptures, we are often guilty of being imperfect interpreters. I shall do the best I can to catch the spirit of the man, Peter, and to determine what God is trying to say to us and reduce the interference to a minimum.

Now, I suppose more people would like me if

I were to declare that I preach the Bible and nothing but the Bible. I attempt to do that, but honesty compels me to say that the best I can do is to preach the Bible as I understand it. I trust that through your prayers and the Spirit of Christ my understanding may be right. If you pray and if I yield and trust, perhaps what we get from First Peter will indeed be approximately what Peter would say if he were here in person. We will stay as close as we can to the Word of the Living God.

Reputation for being first

The man Peter had a reputation for being first because he was a most impetuous man. He was either the first or among the very first in almost everything that took place and that touched him while he was alive.

For this reason, I suppose that Peter would have made a wonderful American! He usually opened his mouth and talked before he thought and that is a characteristic of many of us. He rushed to do what he had to do—and that is also characteristic of us.

From the record of the gospels, it appears that Peter may have been the first, or at least among the very first, to become a disciple of John the Baptist. He was among the first disciples who turned to Jesus when John the Baptist pointed and said, "Look, the Lamb of God, who takes away the sin of the world" (John 1:29b).

Peter was the first apostle called by our Lord to follow Him. I believe that Peter was the first convert for he was the first man to say, "Thou art the Son of the Living God."

Peter was among the very first to see our Lord after He had risen from the dead. There are those who insist that Peter was the first, believing that the Lord Jesus appeared to no one else until after a meeting with His beloved friend, Peter.

Also, remember that Peter was the first of the New Testament preachers. It is quite in keeping with the temperament of this man that when the Holy Spirit had come at Pentecost and there was opportunity for someone to stand and speak the Truth, Peter should be the man to do it.

I think there is no profound theological reason back of this. I think it is a matter of temperament and disposition. When 120 persons are suddenly filled with the Holy Spirit and it falls to the lot of one of them to leap up and express the wonder of what has just happened, it would be normal for the man Peter to be the one. So, he got to his feet and poured out that great sermon recorded in the second chapter of the book of Acts—the great sermon that converted 3,000 persons!

But Peter was a man, and in his early discipleship and ministry there were glaring contradictions and inconsistencies in his life. It is not possible for us to try to boast and say that this man, this second greatest of the apostles, never deviated one inch from the straight line from the moment of his conversion to the time of his death. I do believe in realism in religion and I do not think any good can come from hiding the bad and trying to reflect an unnatural righteousness which is not true to the whole character of the man.

Actually, I wish that every one of us could be like the angels or those strange creatures in the first chapter of Ezekiel, of whom it is said that when they went "they went every one straight forward."

Need to go straight forward

I do not know what that means precisely, but I do know that it is an intriguing test—when they went they went straight forward. I wish that from the time I was converted at the age of 17 I had gone straight forward; but I did not and most of us have not. We zig-zag on our way to heaven in place of flying a straight course. I am sorry about this. I don't excuse it, but I try to understand it!

Well, Peter was a bundle of contradictions and I take the position that it further glorifies the grace of God that He could take a weak and vacillating and inconsistent man like Peter and make Saint Peter out of him!

Read again all that the New Testament says about Peter and you will find glaring contradictions. In His very first meeting with

Peter, Jesus said, " 'You are Simon son of John. You will be called Cephas' (which when translated, Peter [A stone, KJV])" (John 1:42). Jesus Himself in calling Peter gave him this new name meaning a rock, which is of course a solid and unshaking thing.

But this man—this "rock"—was so wavering that he denied his Lord! He clipped off a man's ear in an impatient act to defend his Master, yet within a few hours denied that he had ever met Jesus. He was prone to rush into a situation, to act without thinking, and to apologize often. That was the rock—but a wavering rock—and that in itself is a contradiction!

I note also that Peter was not above rebuking his Lord and Master. He could walk up to Jesus and rebuke Him as though they were equals. But in the next moment, he might be down on his knees in a trembling reverence, crying, "Depart from me, Lord, for I am an unclean man!"

That was Peter—more daring than any of the apostles and often with more faith—but he had more daring than he had faith! Have you met any of God's children like that?

You remember that Peter was so daring that he rushed out of the boat and actually walked on the water, and yet he had such little faith that it would not support his daring. So he sank, and then had to be helped by the Lord to keep him from drowning!

Yes, this man Peter was the first one to con-

fess his Lord and then the first one to deny
Him.

He was the man that Jesus called "Blessed"
and a little later called him Satan. "Blessed are
you, Simon Son of Jonah"; then, "Get behind
me, Satan!" (Matthew 16:17, 23).

I mention a few other contradictions about
the man, Peter. He is said by a portion of the
Christian church to be a vicar of Christ on
earth, and yet Peter himself never seemed to
have found out about it! He never referred to
himself as the vicar or vice-regent of Christ; he
called himself an apostle, one of the elders.
That's all. The humblest elder in any Pres-
byterian church has a title as great as Peter ever
claimed for himself, except that he said he was
one of the apostles.

I could point out that Peter is supposed by
many to have been the first of the popes and
yet he was overshadowed by one of his fellow
apostles, for without question, Paul overshadowed Peter.

Paul was greater

The man Peter was a great man, but the man
Paul was greater. It would seem to me that if
God were to select a pope, the first one, He
would have chosen Paul, the mightiest, the
most intellectual of them all, rather than the
wavering and inconsistent Peter.

I point out, too, that Peter fades out of the
book of Acts and as he does so, Paul moves in.

By the time we come to the end of the Acts, Peter is not visible anywhere. Paul fills the horizon and when God would lay the foundations of His church, forming its doctrines deep and strong, He chose Paul and not Peter.

So, this is a simple and very brief sketch of the man, Peter. Many other things could be said about him, but he is able to speak to us again out of his New Testament letters for he was declared an apostle to the Jews as Paul was to the Gentiles.

The Jews had been scattered abroad and that is the reason for this letter from Peter. They had been dispersed into many nations and at the day of Pentecost, they had come back to Jerusalem, numbering into the hundreds of thousands. Then when Peter preached, they were converted in large numbers, and returning to their own countries, carried the message of the risen Savior and the coming of the Holy Spirit. Thus there were colonies of Christians in all of the provinces of Rome and Peter felt that he was to be pastor to that great number of Jewish Christians scattered abroad. He accepted his apostleship to the Jews most seriously and he wrote his first pastoral letter to the Jewish converts to Christ scattered throughout Roman Asia.

Actually, the circumstances in the Roman provinces that brought forth this letter from Peter were very grievous indeed. The Roman emperors had begun harsh persecution of the

Christians. Jesus had told them that they were to expect persecution and now it was beginning to break over their heads like billows over a sinking ship.

One of the men coming into great political power was the emperor Nero, who is remembered in history as the most incredibly wicked of all the sons of Rome. His life and his acts and his habits are among the most wretched and offensive in all of history so no one can mention in public all the crimes of which he was guilty. But he was the emperor—and Peter and the rest of the Christians were under his control.

It is recorded of Nero that he set the city of Rome on fire and then in his own tower played the harp and sang Greek songs while Rome burned. But then he became frightened, realizing that the Romans would turn on him if they knew he had set the fire, so he looked around for a scapegoat—and who could be easier to blame than the troublesome Christians?

These believers were vocal and they were in evidence everywhere. So, Nero turned on the Christians as Hitler turned on the Jews and he had them slain by the tens of thousands. Property was taken from them, they were thrown into jail, they were tortured in many ways and they were killed—all of this throughout the regions of Bithynia and Pontius and Cappadocia and Roman Asia.

Peter, the dear man of God, knew what was

happening. He had seen some of it himself in the city of Jerusalem and he knew the fury of the persecution. Out of this knowledge came his letter of encouragement, a letter inspired by the Spirit of God as he waited on the Lord in long, amazing hours of prayer for his suffering Christian brothers and sisters.

I think it must be said of Peter that within himself he felt very keenly the loneliness of the "strangers" to whom he wrote. They were scattered, they were persecuted, they were in heaviness, they were isolated in this world for their Christian faith.

The genuine Chistian is a lonely soul

The Christian, the genuine Christian, realizes that he is indeed a lonely soul in the middle of a world which affords him no fellowship. I contend that if the Christian breaks down on occasion and lets himself go in tears, he ought not to feel that he is weak. It is a normal loneliness in the midst of a world that has disowned him. He has to be a lonely man!

Those to whom Peter wrote were strangers in many ways and first of all because they were Jews. They were Jews scattered among the Romans and they never could accept and bow to the Roman ways. They learned the Greek tongue in the world of their day, but they never could learn the Roman ways. They were Jews, a people apart, even as they are today.

Besides that, they had become Christian

believers so they were no longer merely Jews. Their sense of alienation from the world around them had increased and doubled. They were not only Jews—unlike the Gentiles around them—but they were Christians, unlike the Jews as well as unlike the Gentiles!

This is the reason that it is easily possible for a Christian believer to be the loneliest person in the world under a set of certain circumstances. This sense of not belonging is a part of our Christian heritage. That sense of belonging in another world and not belonging to this one steals into the Christian bosom and marks him off as being different from the people around him. Many of our hymns have been born out of that very loneliness, that sense of another and higher citizenship!

Citizenship is in heaven

That is exactly the thing that keeps a Christian separated—knowing that his citizenship is not on earth at all but in heaven above, and that he looks for the Savior to come. Who is there that can look more earnestly for the coming of the Lord Jesus than the one who feels that he is a lonely person in the middle of a lonely world?

Peter loved the Lord Jesus Christ and his letters to suffering believers clearly reveal that great and sweeping changes had come into his life. He had become stable, he had become solid, he had become the steady and dependable servant of Christ. Now he was able to see that suffering for Christ is one of the privileges of Christian life and he prepared his brothers and sisters for the future with his counsel: "Dear friends, do not be surprised at the painful trial you are suffering . . . but rejoice that you participate in the sufferings of Christ" (1 Peter 4:12–13).

Fellow believers, it is the same kind of world in which we live in this 20th century. We do well to let the Apostle Peter speak to us!

No matter who you are, no matter what your education, you can read Peter's First Epistle and understand it reasonably well and you can say to yourself, "The Holy Spirit is saying this to me!"

There isn't anything dated in the Book of God. When I go to my Bible, I find dates but no dating. I mean that I find the sense and the feeling that everything here belongs to me. There is nothing here that is obviously for another age, another time, another people.

Many other volumes and many other books of history contain the passionate outpourings of the minds of men on local situations but we soon find ourselves bored with them. Unless we are actually doing research we do not care that much about something dated, something belonging only to another age.

But when the Holy Spirit wrote the epistles, through Peter and Paul and the rest, He wrote them and addressed them to certain people and then made them so universally applicable that every Christian who reads them today in any part of the world, in any language or dialect, forgets that they were written to someone else and says, "This was addressed to me. The Holy Spirit had me in mind. This is not antiquated and dated. This is the living Truth for me—now! It is just as though God had just heard of my trouble and is speaking to me to help me and encourage me in the time of my distress!"

Brethren, this is why the Bible stays young always. This is why the Word of the Lord God is as fresh as every new sunrise, as sweet and graciously fresh as the dew on the grass the morning after the clear night—because it is God's Word to man!

This is the wonder of divine inspiration and the wonder of the Book of God!

You Can Have the Trappings!

*. . . the God and Father of our Lord
Jesus Christ . . . has given us new birth.*
(1 Peter 1:3)

A professing Christian who finds it necessary to keep on apologizing to this
present world has missed the whole point of
the New Testament revelation of salvation
through our Lord Jesus Christ!

The Apostle Peter says that "[God] has given
us new birth into a living hope." And this constitutes a continuing miracle which should
have put the Christian church on the offensive
forever!

We have no cause to apologize to the world if
we have been born again, changed and transformed through the miracle of supernatural
grace and thus endued with the only living and
eternal hope which has ever come into this sad
and hopeless world!

Why don't we have the courage that belongs to our sound Christian faith? I cannot understand all of this ignoble apologizing and the whipped-dog attitude of so many professing Christians!

I cannot keep from mentioning the kind of confidence and enthusiasm and fascination which the faithful communist holds in his devil-inspired doctrine, and I remind you—communists never apologize!

A real offensive for God

But many Christians spend a lot of time and energy in making excuses, because they have never broken through into a real offensive for God by the unlimited power of the Holy Spirit! The world has nothing that we want—for we are believers in a faith that is as well authenticated as any solid fact of life. The truths we believe and the links in the chain of evidence are clear and rational. I contend that the church has a right to rejoice and that this is no time in the world's history for Christian believers to settle for a defensive holding action!

Brethren, let's not forget that the new birth is a miracle—a major miracle! It is a vital and unique work of God in the human nature. Peter in describing it relates it to the miracle of Jesus Christ rising from the dead, " . . . [God] has given us new birth into a living hope through the resurrection of Jesus Christ from the dead."

So, there is a divine principle here—the fact

that a man truly born again is a man who has experienced regenesis, supernatural regenesis. Just as God generated the heavens and the earth in the beginning, He generates again in the breast of the believing man!

Just as surely as God's calling the world out of nothing was a major miracle, the work of God in making a believing Christian out of a sinner is a major miracle as well.

In the light of what God is willing to do and wants to do, consider how we try to "get them in" in modern Christianity.

We get them in any way we can. Then we try to work on them—to adjust them and to reform them.

I may be misunderstood when I say this, but we even have two works of grace because the first was so apologetically meaningless that we try to have two.

I do not speak against the second work of grace; but I am pleading for the work that ought to be done in a man's heart when he first meets God. What I am asking is this: Why should we be forced to invent some second or third or fourth experience somewhere along the line to obtain what we should have received the first time we met God?

I believe in the anointing of the Holy Spirit after regeneration—but I also believe that we ought not to downgrade the new birth in order to find a place for the anointing of the Holy Spirit.

I have read much and studied long the lives and ministries of many of the old saints of God in past generations. I am inclined to believe that many of them were better Christians when they were just newly-regenerated than the run of the so-called "deeper life" people whom I meet today.

We should expect a miracle

I think the difference is in the emphasis of the major miracle which we ought to expect in genuine Christian conversion. Those old-timers would not have believed if a major miracle had not taken place. They would never have been willing to accept a pale and apologetic kind of believing on the Son of God. They insisted on a miracle taking place within the human breast. They knew what Peter meant when he said that the Lord God has begotten us unto a living hope—and they accepted the principle of a miracle wrought in a human being through divine grace.

In reading the Old Testament, we are reminded again and again of the possibility of this miracle of cleansing and transformation.

"Create in me a pure heart, O God,/ and renew a steadfast spirit within me" (Psalm 51:10)—there you have at least the hint of a miracle within the human being. The Old Testament men of God never told us that they had reasoned themselves into a position of faith and power—but that something had happened within their beings that could not be naturally and fully explained!

In Old Testament times, God plainly said:

> "This is the covenant I will make with the
>   house of Israel
> after that time," declares the Lord.
> "I will put my law in their minds
>   and write it on their hearts.
> I will be their God,
>   and they will be my people."
>   (Jeremiah 31:33)

Again in Ezekiel, God said:

> I will give you a new heart and put a new spirit in you; I will remove from you your heart of stone and will give you a heart of flesh. And I will put my Spirit in you and move you to follow my decrees and be careful to keep my laws. . . . you will be my people, and I will be your God.
>   (36:26–28)

I think you would have to call that a strong hint of regenesis and moral rebirth.

But come along into the New Testament and you will find that it is no longer veiled—the supernatural miracle of the new birth is boldly and openly proclaimed.

The Apostle John writes that our Savior said that if we tried to come to Him and had not been born anew, we could not enter the kingdom of God.

John also plainly reports that ". . . to all who received him, to those who believed in his name, he gave the right to become children of God—children born not of natural descent, nor of human decision or a husband's will but born of God" (John 1:12–13).

The Apostle Paul told the Corinthian church that "if anyone is in Christ, he is a new creation, the old has gone, the new has come!" (2 Corinthians 5:17).

Can you think of any way to make a statement stronger than that?

Peter describes the miracle in his day as being "born again . . . through the living and enduring word of God" (1 Peter 1:23).

In his epistle, James wrote that "[God] chose to give us birth through the word of truth, that we might be a kind of firstfruits of all he created" (1:18).

A miracle of transforming grace

Throughout the New Testament it is made as plain as it can ever be made that God expected to perform a miracle of His transforming grace within the human life of every person willing to come to Him in faith.

If we believe the New Testament we must surely believe that the new birth is a major miracle, as truly a miracle of God as was the first creation, for the new birth is actually the creating of another man in the heart where another man had been.

I believe this is the kind of genuine Christian conversion that we are talking about—the putting of a new man in the old man's place, so that we are born "anew."

This is the point at which I insist that the new birth was provided in the love and grace and wisdom of God in order to draw a sharp line between those who acquire Christianity by any other method and those who have experienced regenesis.

This is a good place for me to comment that some professing Christians are still trying to find natural and reasonable explanations for that which God has said He would do miraculously by His Spirit.

Let me warn you that if you are a Christian believer and you have found a psychologist who can explain to you exactly what happened to you in the matter of your faith, you have been unfrocked! At the very moment that a man's experience in Christ can be broken down and explained by the psychologists, we have just another church member on our hands— and not a believing Christian!

It can't be explained

That is my frank opinion for I am thoroughly convinced that the miraculous element in the genuine Christian experience can never be explained by means of psychological examination. The honest psychologist can only stand off respectfully and say, "Behold the works of the Lord." He never can explain it!

I don't mind telling you that it is my earnest faith that all that is worthwhile in Christianity is a miracle! Actually, I can get along nicely without the outward dressings of Christianity—the trappings and the exterior paraphernalia. I can get along without them because at the heart of our faith are the miracles that throb and beat within the revealed message of God and within the beings of those who truly believe—and that's about all there is to the Christian faith!

As far as I am concerned, I believe that supernatural grace has been the teaching and the experience of the Christian church from Pentecost to the present hour!

Now, to be genuinely born again is the miracle of becoming a partaker of the divine nature. It is more than just a religious expression; more than the hyphenated adjective we often hear, such as "He's a born-again man."

Some evangelicals are slow to admit it, but I know that this important matter of the new birth has fallen into cold hands, along with many other important Bible teachings. I don't have to tell you that in many Christian churches you will feel as though you are in a mortuary instead of the church of the Living God.

Christians who have been miraculously begotten again ought to be rejoicing in their deliverance from the tomb of spiritual death. Instead, we often feel as though we are in the presence of a corpse just brought in from the street. Sad indeed that the words "born again" have become words that seem to mean precious little because the emphasis of supernatural grace has dwindled away, even in some fundamentalist circles.

The new birth is still a miracle of God—it is not a matter of the mind, not just a mental thing. It is my judgment that there are many who talk about being born again on the basis of their mental assent to Christian principles. I think there are many who have received Christ mentally who have never discovered the supernatural quality of the grace of God or of the acts of God.

Must be the most amazing people

God fully expects the church of Jesus Christ to prove itself a miraculous group in the midst of a hostile world. Christians of necessity must be in contact with the world but in being and spirit ought to be separated from the world— and as such, we should be the most amazing people in the world.

However, we have watered down the miracle of divine grace to a point where you actually must find a name on the record books to know whether an individual is a Christian or not.

Brethren, there is a difference! There is also a sad and terrible day of judgment yet to come, a day of revelation and shock for those who have depended upon a mental assent to Christianity instead of the miracle of the new birth!

It is only through the illumination of the new birth that we humans come to a full understanding of the word *hope* as Peter has used it in his epistles.

I like to think of *hope* as being one of the great words that Christ gave us even though it was used in the Old Testament and is actually used 140 times in the Bible.

But haven't you noticed in the New Testament that Jesus Christ made no effort to coin new words, novel words? He used words that are well-known, but He invariably charged these words with a new and wonderful meaning. That is why we find ourselves looking back to His expressions and then saying, "Jesus gave us that word!"

In that sense and understanding, we may well say that hope is a word which has taken on a new and deeper meaning for us because the Savior took it into His mouth. Loving Him and obeying Him, we suddenly discover that hope is really the direction taken by the whole Bible. Hope is the music of the whole Bible, the heartbeat, the pulse and the atmosphere of the whole Bible.

Hope means a desirable expectation, a pleasurable anticipation. As men know this word, it often blows up in our faces and often cruelly disappoints us as human beings. Hope that is only human will throw us down and wound us just as pleasurable anticipation often turns to discouragement or sorrow.

Christian hope is alive

But Peter assures us that the Christian hope is alive, that the Christian is begotten again—born again—unto a living hope. This English word for *lively* or *living* is the strongest word in the Bible for life, and is the word used of God Himself when it says He is the Living God.

So, in this way, God takes a Christian hope and touches it with Himself and imparts His own meaning of life to the hope of the believers!

There is a great lesson here for any Christian believer who has settled down into the present earthly situation and is becoming satisfied with many good things he can now afford and is able to enjoy.

It is safe to say that the pleasurable anticipation of the better things to come has almost died out in the church of Christ. It is a great temptation to take the shallow view that we do not need any heaven promised for tomorrow because we are so well situated here and now.

This is the emphasis of our day: "We don't need to hope—we have it now!"

But the modern emphasis is wretched and it is wrong. When we do talk about the future we talk about eschatology instead of heaven. When I find any Christian who can live and

work and serve here and snuggle down into
the world like your hand fits into an old and
familiar glove, I worry about him. I must
wonder if he has ever truly been born again.

Brethren, we are still living in a wicked and
adulterous generation and I must confess that
the Christians I meet who really amount to
something for the Savior are very much out of
key and out of tune with their generation.

You may not agree with me, but I must
believe that when God works a miracle within
the human breast, heaven becomes the Christian's home immediately, and he is drawn to it
as the bird in the springtime is drawn to fly
north to its summer homeland.

The trusting Christian has a homeland, too;
but the fact that we are not anticipating it and
not looking forward to it with any pleasure is a
most telling and serious sign that something is
wrong with our spiritual life!

I recall a recent poll in which it was reported
that 82 percent of the American people expressed a belief in God and the expectation of
going to heaven. Personally, I do not like to
deal in percentages, but from what I know personally of American men and women I should
like boldly and bluntly to say that I will guess
that about three-fourths of that 82 percent are
indulging an invalid hope.

It is sad, but it must be said that the earthly
hope of men and women without God and
without Christ and without faith is a vain

hope. Certainly there is a great company of people all around us needing the reminder that if they are going to go to heaven they had better begin to live like it now and if they expect to die like a Christian they had better live like a Christian now.

World's hope is vague and in vain

The hope held by the worldling is vague and it is held in vain because of unbelief. It is unbelief that prevents our minds from soaring into the celestial city and walking by faith with God along the golden streets. It is unbelief that keeps us narrowly tied down here, looking eagerly and anxiously to the newspaper ads to find out who is coming to preach because we feel like we need to have our spirit cheered up.

Anyone who needs to be chucked under the chin all the time to keep him happy and satisfied is in bad shape spiritually. He can ignore the fact that the Bible urges us to go on unto perfection for he is of that part of the church that cannot be satisfied without a visit from the latest gospel peddler, who promises cowbells, a musical hand-saw and a lot of other novelties!

Brethren, we have been born of God and our Christian hope is a valid hope! No emptiness, no vanity, no dreams that cannot come true. Your expectation should rise and you should challenge God and begin to dream high dreams of faith and spiritual attainment and expect God to meet them. You cannot out-hope

God and you cannot out-expect God. Remember that all of your hopes are finite, but all of God's ability is infinite!

Now, brethren, what is it that makes our Christian hope a living hope and gives it reality and substance for the future?

The answer is clear and plain—the resurrection of our Lord Jesus Christ is God's gracious guarantee of our blessed future.

I dare to say this to you, my friends—your Christian hope is just as good as Jesus Christ. Your anticipation for the future lives or dies with Jesus. If He is who He said He was, you can spread your wings and soar. If He is not, you will fall to the ground like a lump of lead.

Jesus Christ is our hope and God has raised Him from the dead and since Jesus overcame the grave, Christians dare to die.

Centuries ago unbelieving men thought they could stamp out the Christian gospel by parading those transformed, born-again followers of Jesus to the places of their violent torture and executions. Soon the unfeeling executioners began to feel something in the presence of joyful victory over death and they passed along this word: "Behold how these Christians die!"

I contend that they were able to die well because they had lived well and I think that the man who has not lived well will have a tough time getting in.

In our day, that statement will shock some of our "nickel-in-the-slot" theologians—those who insist that salvation is like putting a nickel in the slot of faith. Just pull down the lever and take eternal life which you cannot lose—and walk away!

The resurrection of Jesus Christ is our guarantee and a Christian dares to die if he has lived right and has a hope that is living and has been born of the Spirit and is walking with God!

CHAPTER

4

Never Apologize for God's Mercy!

Praise be to the God and Father of our
Lord Jesus Christ! In his great mercy . . .
(1 Peter 1:3)

There are many in our day who seem to hold to an idea that God deals with some people in mercy and with others in justice.

However, the Bible really leaves no room for doubt about this matter—it is plain that God deals with all men in mercy and that every benefit God bestows is according to mercy!

If God had not dealt with us all in mercy, we would have perished before we could have had time to be converted.

I like to think of it in this way—we float on the vast, limitless sea of divine mercy for it is the mercy of God that sustains the worst sinner.

If we have protection, it is according to the mercy of God. If we have food and sustenance, it is of God's mercy. If we have providence to guide us, it is surely in the mercy of God.

David once cried out to the Lord, "have mercy upon me and hear my prayer!"

Was he just using words for the sounds of words? No, of course not, for mercy surely enters into the hearing of prayer. David's cry is a sound, clear, logical statement of theological fact. Mercy must enter into the holiest act that any man can ever perform and it is a constant mercy on the part of God.

The fact that I am sane instead of committed to an institution is an act of mercy on God's part. The fact that I am free and not in prison is due to the mercy of God. The fact that I am alive and not dead is God's mercy over me—and the same for you!

It is true for all men, Jew or Gentile or Muslim, whether they believe it or not. We ought to thank God for some knowledge and some comprehension of this great sea—the mercy of God!

Early in his first epistle the Apostle Peter blessed God, the Father of our Lord Jesus Christ, because of His abundant mercy towards those who believe and are begotten again.

Now, before we look at that adjective abundant, I want to point out that when Peter broke forth into that doxology he was not simply having himself a "spiritual time." He was not just simply letting himself go as it was said of the little old lady at camp meeting.

The Spirit-led life is a clear, logical and rational life. There were particularly sound theological reasons for Peter saying, "Blessed be the Lord!" He blessed God because He has begotten us again and because it was through His abundant mercy that He did it and through it all that we might have a living hope, not a dead one!

Not according to whim or impulse

I point out that the Spirit-led Christian life is not according to whim or impulse and yet there are Christians who feel that you cannot be spiritual without being capricious and that the more impulsive you are the more spiritual you are.

Years ago there was a popular healing evangelist who boasted that he was too busy running around to plan anything very well. So he just sort of stumbled into the meetings and muddled through them. As a result, he was advertised as a "man of lightning changes." No one ever knew whether the service would open with a hymn, with the offering, or with the sermon.

Personally, I am not sure about "men of lightning changes." It may be a matter of temperament, or it could be a cover-up for laziness and poor planning and lack of thought. My feeling is that men who depend upon capricious action and impulsive whims usually are not much good in the church of Christ and they wouldn't be any good if they worked for Ford or General Motors, either.

Why do I say that? Because I want to emphasize the manner in which the apostles were Spirit-led. They were not known as men of rash and impulsive moods, constantly changing decisions and judgments. Led by the Spirit of God, they wanted always to do what God wanted them to do. As a result, the things that God wanted them to do always seemed to fit perfectly into the total scheme of redemption and the whole will of God in the New Testament!

This allows me to say that Peter was of little use to God until he got the victory over being whimsical and temperamental and impulsive. While he was still temperamental, scolding the Lord of Glory for this or that, he was of very little use to the Lord. He was almost a total loss.

But when Peter was filled with the Holy Spirit and received a divine vision and began to suffer for Jesus' sake, he got leveled down and became the great apostle, second only to Paul in the New Testament. But God had to take those lightning changes out of Peter and stabilize him in the harness where he would work effectively and fruitfully for the Lord.

A logical link

So, there is a clear answer for those who feel that if they are not acting strangely, they are not spiritual and if an action isn't capricious, it cannot be of the Holy Spirit. The answer is this—we always find a clear, logical link between everything the apostles said in the New Testament and their reasons for saying it! That's true, always!

It should be that way in our Christian churches, too. We are not to be victims of caprice, the weather, the state of our health or whether or not we just happen to feel like praying.

We need to assemble ourselves together as believers whether the weather is good or bad. We have to pray and draw nigh unto the Lord whether we feel like it or not. Reading Peter's letter to those early Christians, we realize that they were living for Jesus regardless of circumstances or their mood.

A high level

Actually, there are very few Christians among us who can testify that their spiritual moods are always at a high, sustained level.

A Christian brother will say to me in private: "Brother Tozer, I believe I am a Spirit-filled man. My all is on the altar as far as I know. But I need advice and help about my weakness—I don't always have the same degree of feeling and spirituality. Sometimes I am up and sometimes I am down! What can I do about it?"

I am forced to reply in frankness: "I wish you could tell me because I do not know the answer! I do not know of any truly honest

Christian that can get up and say, 'I live at a consistently high level! I fly at an altitude of 30,000 feet all the way!' "

If any of you can honestly say that you have never ceased from that high level in your Christian experience, you are blessed and I honor you!

Live according to spiritual truth

Brethren, we are not plugging for the necessity of an up-and-down Christian experience. I mean to say that we are men and women who are to live according to the high logic of spiritual truth, not according to our feelings and moods.

Some of the old fathers in the faith talked about a frame—they would put an entry in their diary: "Was of a very happy frame this morning." Perhaps later there was an entry: "Was of a very low frame this morning. Felt very depressed." Nothing has changed except their "frame." We say it a little differently, for we say "frame of mind." The song writer was actually saying: "I dare not trust the sweetest frame of mind, but wholly lean on Jesus' name!"

So you see, brethren, you and I live for God according to a holy, high spiritual logic and not according to shifting and changing frames of mind or moods. Amen!

Some would not want me to put it like that; they would call it a very unspiritual doctrine.

"You have got to be blessed all the time," they say. Happy, happy, happy!

But if they would just quit fibbing and tell the truth, they would admit that there are days when they are not as "happy, happy" as they were the day before. The great remedy for us all is to remember the abundant mercy of God, read God's Word and pray, sing a song and take the means of grace and we will find ourselves satisfied in the Lord, as we ought to be!

So, all that He is doing for us is according to His mercy, His abundant mercy.

This word *abundant* comes from a Greek word which means very large, very great, the largest number. It means much and it means many—it can mean all of these things. According to His largest number, His very large, very great, many mercies, God has begotten us again.

The word *abundant* is not really sufficient because everything God has is unlimited. Because He is the Infinite God, everything about Him is infinite which means that it has no boundary in any direction. I know that is hard for us to comprehend.

I remember preaching an entire sermon on "The Infinitude of God" and I recall that only one man ever spoke to me about it and told me that he had gotten the point of my sermon. So far as I know, everyone else just wrote that one off. But this concept is something that we must recognize even if it hurts our heads. We must come to this knowledge that God is infinite, unlimited, boundless, with no sign post anywhere in the universe saying "this is the end."

No need to enlarge adjectives

We do not need any enlarging adjectives when we speak of God, or of His love or mercy. God Almighty fills the universe and overfills it because it is His character—infinite and unlimited!

We do not need to say God's great love, although we do say it.

When we say God's mercy we do not need to say God's abundant mercy, although we do say it. The reason we say it is to cheer and elevate our own thoughts of God—not to infer that there is any degree in the mercy of God.

Actually, when we use the expression, "the mercy of God," we are referring to that which is so vast that the word *vast* does not begin to describe it for we are talking about that which has no limits anywhere, that which has its center anywhere and its circumference nowhere.

Our adjectives can be useful only when we talk about earthly things—when we refer to the great love of a man for his family or we talk about little faith or great faith or more faith or much faith.

We talk about wealth and we speak of a man who has considerable wealth. Another man may represent very great wealth and a person who really made it is a man of fabulous wealth. So we can go up and down the scale from considerable to fabulous because men have ways of measuring what they hold in material things.

But then we come to God—and there can be no such measuring point, no such evaluation. When we speak of the riches of God we must include all the riches there are. God is not less rich or more rich—He is rich—He holds all things in His being!

So it is with mercy. God is not less merciful or more merciful—He is full of mercy, for whatever God is, He is in the fullness of unlimited grace.

So, the word *abundant* is not used here for God—it is put in here for us! It is used to elevate our minds to the consideration of the unlimited vastness of the mercy of God.

Brethren, this all boils down to a simple statement: "God's mercies are equal to God Himself." For that reason alone all comparisons are futile. If you want to know how merciful God is, discover how great He is and you will know!

I recall a true story told us by Rev. D.C. Kopp, missionary to Africa, on one of his furloughs from the Congo. He described the office of deacon in the national church and told of a fine stalwart Christian brother who had the job of disciplining the converts.

One young convert was proving to be a

source of real trouble in the church because he was inclined to break the rules and do the things that a Christian brother should not do.

After he had been disciplined many times, this concerned deacon called in the erring brother once more and told him frankly, "Now, brother, you have been failing us and disappointing us and disgracing your Christian calling and it is about enough! When we started dealing with you we had a bottle of forgiveness, but I am here to tell you that that bottle is just about empty! We are just about through with you!"

The missionary got a chuckle out of that incident for he thought it was a quaint and picturesque way to let the brother know that he was no longer passing inspection. But, on the other hand, it is far from being a demonstration of God's dealing with us for the bottle of God's forgiveness has neither top nor bottom!

God has never yet said to a man, "The bottle of my mercy is just about empty!"

God acting the way He acts

Let us be thankful that God's mercy does not run out of a bottle. God's mercy is God acting the way He acts towards people—therefore, we can say it is abundant mercy.

Now, when does a person really become aware of this great sea of the mercy of God?

When by faith we come across the threshold into the kingdom of God we recognize and identify it and God's mercy becomes as sweet and blessed as though it were all brand new. It is through His abundant mercy that we are begotten again, but it is that same broad stream from God that kept and preserved the sinner, even through 50 or 60 years of presumption and rebellion.

My father was 60 years old when he bowed before Jesus Christ and was born again. That was a near lifetime of 60 years through which he had sinned and lied and cursed. But when he gave his heart to the Lord Jesus Christ and was converted, the mercy of God that saved him and took him to heaven was no greater than the mercy of God that had kept him and endured him for 60 years.

There is an old story that fits perfectly here about the Jewish rabbi centuries ago who consented to take a weary traveler into his house for a night's rest.

After they had eaten together, the rabbi said, "You are a very old man, are you not?"

"Yes," the traveler replied, "I am almost a century old."

As they talked, the rabbi brought up the matter of religion and asked the visitor about his faith and about his relation to God.

"Oh, I do not believe in God," the aged man replied. "I am an atheist."

The rabbi was infuriated. He arose and opened the door and ordered the man from his house.

"I cannot keep an atheist in my house over-night," he reasoned.

The weary old man said nothing but hobbled to the door and stepped out into the darkness. The rabbi again sat down by his candle and Old Testament, when it seemed he heard a voice saying, "Son, why did you turn that old man out?"

"I turned him out because he is an atheist and I cannot endure him overnight!"

But then the voice of God said, "Son, I have endured him almost 100 years—don't you think you could endure him for one night?"

The rabbi leaped from his chair, rushed into the darkness and, overtaking the older man, brought him back into the house and then treated him like a long lost brother.

God's mercy has endured

It was the mercy of God that has endured the atheist for nearly 100 years. It was the mercy of God that endured my father as a sinner for 60 years. The mercy of God endured me through the first 17 years of my life and has brought me through all of the years since. The Bible plainly declares that God deals with all of us in mercy and that He never violates mercy, for David testifies that, "The Lord is good to all: and his tender mercies are over all his works!" (Psalm 145:9, KJV).

Any idea people may have that God works according to one facet of His nature one day and according to another facet the next day is all wrong. I repeat again—God never violates any facet of His nature in dealing with men.

When God sent Judas Iscariot to hell He did not violate mercy and when God forgave Peter it was not in violation of justice. Everything that God does is with the full protection of all of His infinite attributes. That is why a sinner may live to be 100 years old and sin against God every moment of his life and still be a partaker of the mercy of God. He still floats on the sea of mercy and it is because of the mercy of God that he is not consumed.

However, brethren, we know there will be a day when the sinner will pass from this realm where God's mercy supports him. He will hear a voice saying, "Depart from me, you that work iniquity, for I never knew you!" Hell will be the justly apportioned abode of those who refuse redeeming mercy even though there has been a providential mercy at work on their behalf throughout their lives.

We Christians should realize, also, that we do not come through the door of mercy and then expect to live apart from the door. We are in the very room of mercy and the sanctuary is a sanctuary of mercy. We must not become self-righteous and imagine we are living such wonderful lives that God blesses us because we are good. That is not so!

God blesses us because of His abundant mercy, the mercy which He has bestowed upon us, and not because of any of our goodness. I do not believe that heaven itself will ever permit us to forget that we are recipients of the goodness of God and for that reason I do not believe that you and I will ever be permitted to forget Calvary.

Another thing in this regard is that although God wants His people to be holy as He is holy, He does not deal with us according to the degree of our holiness but according to the abundance of His mercy. Honesty requires us to admit this.

Believe in justice and judgment

We do believe in justice and we do believe in judgment. We believe the only reason mercy triumphs over judgment is that God, by a divine, omniscient act of redemption, fixed it so man could escape justice and live in the sea of mercy. The justified man, the man who believes in Jesus Christ, born anew and now a redeemed child of God, lives in that mercy always.

The unjust man, however—the unrepentant sinner—lives in it now in a lesser degree, but the time will come when he will face the judgment of God. Though he had been kept by the mercy of God from death, from insanity, from disease, he can violate that mercy, turn his back on it and walk into judgment. Then it is too late!

Let us pray with humility and repentance for

we stand in the mercy of God. I heard of a man who had learned the Ten Commandments so when he prayed he said, "Now, God, I admit I have broken Number One and Number Three and Number Four and Number Seven, but remember, Father, I have kept Number Two and Number Five and Number Six and Number Ten!"

How unutterably foolish—that as men we should appeal to God and try to dicker with Him and portion out our goodness like a storekeeper! What an example we have set for us by the life and faith of the old Puritan saint, Thomas Hooker, as his death approached.

Those around his beside said, "Brother Hooker, you are going to receive your reward."

"No, no!" he breathed. "I go to receive mercy!"

What an example for us, because Brother Hooker rated very high in the ranks of holy men in the Body of Christ, yet he did not leave this life looking for a reward but still looking for the mercy of God!

Look away to the Lord

Brethren, may I just say that if you have been looking at yourself—look away to the Lord of abundant mercy. Fixing yourself over and trying to straighten yourself out will not be sufficient—you must come as you are!

Paul Rader once told about the artist who had an idea for a powerful painting, depicting the plight of a tramp, a human derelict off the street.

He went to the Skid Row district and found just the subject he had in mind—a man who was dirty, disheveled, rundown at the heels, in rags, and completely at home among the disreputable elements of the city.

"I will pay you a fee if you will come to my studio tomorrow morning," the artist told him.

The bum's face brightened and his eyes took on a new light and he said, "You mean you want to put me in a picture?"

"Yes, I want to paint you into a picture and I will give you 50 dollars right now," the artist said. "Just show up at my house tomorrow morning and I will tell you what to do."

But when the artist's doorbell rang the next morning, the painter hardly recognized the man who stood there. He had been shaved, he had on a white shirt and his pants had a reasonable facsimile of a press.

"I don't want to come to your fine place looking like a bum, so I spent the money getting myself cleaned up and fixed up," the man said with pride.

"But I cannot use you now for the painting I had in mind," the artist told him. "I thought you would come just as you were."

Jesus told about two men who went up into the temple to pray.

One said, "God, here I am. I am all fixed up—every hair is in place."

The other said, "Oh God, I just crawled in off Skid Row. Have mercy upon me!" God forgave the Skid Row bum, but sent the other man away, hardened and unrepentant and unforgiven!

We come to Him just as we are but in humble repentance, for when the human spirit comes to God feeling that it is better and more acceptable than others, it automatically shuts itself away from God's presence. But when the human spirit comes to God knowing that anything it receives will be of mercy, then repentance has done its proper work! God promises to forgive and bless that man and take him into His heart and teach him that all of God's kindnesses are due to His mercy.

What more can a sinner ask?

CHAPTER

5

Holiness Is Not
an Option!

*. . . as he who called you is holy, so be
holy in all you do; for it is written:
"Be holy, because I am holy."*
(1 Peter 1:15–16)

Y ou cannot study the Bible diligently and
earnestly without being struck by an obvious fact—the whole matter of personal holiness is highly important to God!

Neither do you have to give long study to the
attitudes of modern Christian believers to dis-
cern that by and large we consider the expression of true Christian holiness to be just a
matter of personal option: "I have looked it
over and considered it, but I don't buy it!"

I have always liked the word *exhort* better
than *command* so I remind you that Peter has
given every Christian a forceful extortation to
holiness of life and conversation. He clearly
bases this exhortation on two great facts—first,

61

the character of God, and second, the command of God.

His argument comes out so simply that we
sophisticates stumble over it—God's children
ought to be holy because God Himself is holy!
We so easily overlook the fact that Peter was an
apostle and he is here confronting us with the
force of an apostolic injunction, completely in
line with the Old Testament truth concerning
the person and character of God and also in
line with what the Lord Jesus had taught and
revealed to His disciples and followers.

Personally, I am of the opinion that we who
claim to be apostolic Christians do not have the
privilege of ignoring such apostolic injunctions.
I do not mean that a pastor can forbid or that a
church can compel. I only mean that morally
we dare not ignore this commandment, "Be
holy."

We cannot ignore it

Because it is an apostolic word, we must face
up to the fact that we will have to deal with it
in some way, and not ignore it—as some Christians do.

Certainly no one has provided us with an
opinion in this matter. Who has ever given us
the right or the privilege to look into the Bible
and say, "I am willing to consider this matter
and if I like it, I will buy it"—using the language of the day.

There is something basically wrong with our

Christianity and our spirituality if we can care-
lessly presume that if we do not like a Biblical
doctrine and choose not to "buy" it, there is no
harm done.

Commandments which we have received
from our Lord or from the apostles cannot be
overlooked or ignored by earnest and committed Christians. God has never instructed us
that we should weigh His desires for us and
His commandments to us in the balances of our
own judgment and then decide what we want
to do about them.

A professing Christian may say, "I have
found a place of real Christian freedom; these
things just don't apply to me."

Of course you can walk out on it! God has
given every one of us the power to make our
own choices. I am not saying that we are forced
to bow our necks to this yoke and we do not
have to apply it to ourselves. It is true that if
we do not like it, we can turn our backs on it.

The record in the New Testament is plain on
this point—many people followed Jesus for a
while and then walked away from Him.

Once Jesus said to His disciples: "Unless you
eat the flesh of the Son of Man and drink his
blood, you have no life in you" (John 6:53).
Many looked at one another and then walked
away from Him.

Jesus turned to those remaining and said,
"You do not want to leave too, do you?" (6:67).

Peter gave the answer which is still my

answer today: "Lord, to whom shall we go? You have words of eternal life" (6:68).

Those were wise words, indeed, words born of love and devotion.

Forced to make a choice

So, we are not forced to obey in the Christian life, but we are forced to make a choice at many points in our spiritual maturity.

We have that power within us to reject God's instruction—but where else shall we go? If we refuse His words, which way will we turn? If we turn away from the authority of God's Word, to whose authority do we yield? Our mistake is that we generally turn to some other human—a man with breath in his nostrils.

I am old-fashioned about the Word of God and its authority. I am committed to believe that if we ignore it or consider this commandment optional, we jeopardize our souls and earn for ourselves severe judgment to come.

Now, brethren, I have said that the matter of holiness is highly important to God. I have personally counted in an exhaustive concordance and found that the word *holiness* occurs 650 times in the Bible. I have not counted words with a similar meaning in English, such as *sanctify* and *sanctified*, so the count would jump nearer to a thousand if we counted these other words with the same meaning.

This word *holy* is used to describe the character of angels, the nature of heaven and the character of God. It is written that angels are holy and those angels who gaze down upon the scenes of mankind are called the watchers and holy ones.

It is said that heaven is a holy place where no unclean thing can enter in. God Himself is described by the adjective *holy*—Holy Ghost, Holy Lord and Holy Lord God Almighty. These words are used of God throughout the Bible, showing that the highest adjective that can be ascribed to God, the highest attribute that can be ascribed to God is that of holiness, and, in a relative sense, even the angels in heaven partake of the holiness of God.

We note in the Bible, too, that the absence of holiness is given as a reason for not seeing God. I am aware of some of the grotesque interpretations which have been given to the text, "Without holiness no one will see the Lord" (Hebrews 12:14b). My position is this: I will not throw out this Bible text just because some people have misused it to support their own patented theory about holiness. This text does have a meaning and it ought to disturb us until we have discovered what it means and how we may meet its conditions.

What does holiness really mean?

What does this word *holiness* really mean? Is it a negative kind of piety from which so many people have shied away?

No, of course not! Holiness in the Bible

means moral wholeness—a positive quality which actually includes kindness, mercy, purity, moral blamelessness and godliness. It is always to be thought of in a positive, white intensity of degree. Whenever it is written that God is holy it means that God is kind, merciful, pure and blameless in a white, holy intensity of degree. When used of men, it does not mean absolute holiness as it does of God, but it is still the positive intensity of the degree of holiness—and not negative.

This is why true Bible holiness is positive—a holy man can be trusted. A holy man can be tested. People who try to live by a negative standard of piety, a formula that has been copyrighted by other humans, will find that their piety does not stand up in times of difficult testing.

Genuine holiness can be put into the place of testing without fear. Whenever there is a breakdown of holiness, that is proof there never was any real degree of holiness in the first place.

Personally, I truly have been affected in my heart by reading the testimonies and commentaries of humble men of God whom I consider to be among the great souls of Christian church history.

I have learned from them that the word and idea of holiness as originally used in the Hebrew did not have first of all the moral connotation. It did not mean that God first of all was pure, for that was taken for granted!

The original root of the word *holy* was of something beyond, something strange and mysterious and awe-inspiring. When we consider the holiness of God we talk about something heavenly, full of awe, mysterious and fear-inspiring. Now, this is supreme when it relates to God, but it is also marked in men of God and deepens as men become more like God.

It is a sense of awareness of the other world, a mysterious quality and difference that has come to rest upon some men—that is a holiness. Now, if a man should have that sense and not be morally right, then I would say that he is experiencing a counterfeit of the devil.

Whenever Satan has reason to fear a truth very gravely, he produces a counterfeit. He will try to put that truth in such a bad light that the very persons who are most eager to obey it are frightened away from it. Satan is very sly and very experienced in the forming of parodies of truth which he fears the most, and then pawns his parody off as the real thing and soon frightens away the serious-minded saints.

I regret to say that some who have called themselves by a kind of copyrighted name of holiness have allowed the doctrine to harden into a formula which has become a hindrance to repentance, for this doctrine has been invoked to cover up frivolity and covetousness, pride and worldliness.

I have seen the results. Serious, honest persons have turned away from the whole idea of holiness because of those who have claimed it and then lived selfish and conceited lives.

But, brethren, we are still under the holy authority of the apostolic command. Men of God have reminded us in the Word that God does ask us and expect us to be holy men and women of God, because we are the children of God, who is holy. The doctrine of holiness may have been badly and often wounded—but the provision of God by His pure and gentle and loving Spirit is still the positive answer for those who hunger and thirst for a life and spirit well-pleasing to God.

When a good man with this special quality and mysterious Presence is morally right and walking in all the holy ways of God and carries upon himself without even knowing it the fragrance of a kingdom that is supreme above the kingdoms of this world, I am ready to accept that as being of God and from God!

The illustration of Moses

By way of illustration, remember that Moses possessed these marks and qualities when he came down from the mount. He had been there with God 40 days and 40 nights—and when he came back everyone could tell where he had been. The lightning still played over his countenance, the glory of the Presence remained. This strange something which men cannot pin down or identify was there.

I lament that this mysterious quality of holy Presence has all but forsaken the earth in our day. Theologians long ago referred to it as the numinous, meaning that overplus of something that is more than righteous, but is righteous in a fearful, awe inspiring, wondrous, heavenly sense. It is as though it is marked with a brightness, glowing with a mysterious fire.

We have reduced God to our terms

I have commented that this latter quality has all but forsaken the earth and I think the reason is very obvious. We are men who have reduced God to our own terms. In the context of the Christian church, we are now told to "gossip" the gospel and "sell" Jesus to people!

We still talk about righteousness, but we are lacking in that bright quality, that numinous which is beyond description.

This mysterious fire was in the bush as you will remember from the Old Testament. A small fire does not frighten people unless it spreads and gets out of control. We are not afraid of fire in that sense, yet we read how Moses, kneeling beside a bush where a small fire burned, hid his face for he was afraid! He had met that mysterious quality. He was full of awe in that manifested Presence.

Later, alone in the mountain and at the sounding of a trumpet, Moses shook, and said, "I am fearfully afraid, and quake."

We are drawn again and again to that

Shekinah that was over Israel for it sums up wonderfully this holiness of God's Presence. There was the overhanging cloud not made of water vapor, not casting a shadow anywhere, mysterious.

As the light of day would begin to fade, that cloud began to turn incandescent and when the darkness had settled, it shone brightly like one vast light hanging over Israel.

Every tent in that diamond-shaped encampment was fully lighted by the strange Shekinah that hung over it. No man had built that fire. No one added any fuel—no one stoked or controlled it. It was God bringing Himself within the confines of the human eye and shining down in His Presence over Israel.

I can imagine a mother taking her little child by the hand to walk through the encampment.

I am sure she would kneel down and whisper to the little fellow: "I want to show you something wonderful. Look! Look at that!"

Probably the response would be: "What is it, Mama?"

Then she would reply in a hushed voice: "That is God—God is there! Our leader Moses saw that fire in the bush. Later, he saw that fire in the mountain. Since we left Egypt that fire of God has followed us and hovered over us all through these years."

"But how do you know it is God, Mama?"

"Because of the Presence in that fire, the mysterious Presence from another world."

This Shekinah, this Presence, had no particular connotation of morality for Israel—that was all taken for granted. It did hold the connotation and meaning of reverence and awe, the solemn and inspiring, different and wonderful and glorious—all of that was there as it was also in the temple.

Then it came down again at Pentecost—that same fire sitting upon each of them—and it rested upon them with an invisible visibility. If there had been cameras, I do not think those tongues of fire could have been photographed—but they were there. It was the sense of being in or surrounded by this holy element, and so strong was it that in Jerusalem when the Christians gathered on Solomon's porch, the people stood off from them as wolves will stand away from a bright camp fire. They looked on, but the Bible says "no one else dared join them" (Acts 5:13a).

Why? Were they held back by any prohibition or restriction?

No one had been warned not to come near these praying people, humble and harmless, clean and undefiled. But the crowd could not come. They could not rush in and trample the place down. They stood away from Solomon's porch because they had sensed a holy quality, a mysterious and holy Presence within this company of believers.

Later, when Paul wrote to the Corinthian Christians to explain the mysterious fullness of the Holy Spirit of God, he said: "Some of you, when you meet together and you hear and obey God, know there is such a sense of God's presence that the unbelievers fall on their faces and then go out and report that God is with you indeed."

Now, that kind of Presence emanates from God as all holiness emanates from God.

If we are what we ought to be in Christ and by His Spirit, if the whole sum of our lives beginning with the inner life is becoming more Godlike and Christlike, I believe something of that divine and mysterious quality and Presence will be upon us.

Saints with holy brightness

I have met a few of God's saints who appeared to have this holy brightness upon them, but they did not know it because of their humility and gentleness of spirit. I do not hesitate to confess that my fellowship with them has meant more to me than all of the teaching I have ever received. I do stand deeply indebted to every Bible teacher I have had through the years, but they did little but instruct my head. The brethren I have known who had this strange and mysterious quality and awareness of God's Person and Presence instructed my heart.

Do we understand what a gracious thing it is to be able to say of a man, a brother in the Lord, "He is truly a man of God"? He doesn't have to tell us that, but he lives quietly and confidently day by day with the sense of this mysterious, awe-inspiring Presence that comes down on some people and means more than all the glib tongues in the world!

Actually, I am afraid of all the glib tongues. I am afraid of the man who can always flip open his Bible and answer every question—he knows too much! I am afraid of the man who has thought it all out and has a dozen epigrams he can quote, the answers which he has thought up over the years to settle everything spiritual. Brethren, I'm afraid of it!

There is a silence that can be more eloquent than all human speech. Sometimes there is a confusion of face and bowing of the head that speaks more divine truth than the most eloquent preacher can impart.

So, Peter reminds us that it is the Lord who has said: "Be holy, because I am holy" (1 Peter 1:16).

First, bring your life into line morally so that God can make it holy; then bring your spiritual life into line that God may settle upon you with the Holy Ghost—with that quality of the Wonderful and the Mysterious and the Divine.

You do not cultivate it and you do not even know it, but it is there and it is this quality of humility invaded by the Presence of God which the church of our day lacks. Oh, that we might yearn for the knowledge and Presence of God in our lives from moment to moment, so that without human cultivation and without toilsome seeking there would come upon us this enduement that gives meaning to our witness! It is a sweet and radiant fragrance and I suggest that in some of our churches it may be strongly sensed and felt.

Now that I have said that, I had better stop and predict that some will ask me, "You don't go by your feelings, do you, Mr. Tozer?"

Well, I do not dismiss the matter of feeling and you can quote me on that if it is worth it!

Feeling is an organ of knowledge and I do not hesitate to say so. Feeling is an organ of knowledge.

To develop this, will you define the word *love* for me?

I don't believe you can actually define love—you can describe it but you cannot define it. A person or a group of people or a race which has never heard of the word *love* can never come to an understanding of what love is even if they could memorize the definitions in all of the world's dictionaries.

But just consider what happens to any simple, freckled-faced boy with his big ears and his red hair awry when he first falls in love. All at once he knows more about love than all of the dictionaries put together!

This is what I am saying—love can only be understood by the feeling of it. The same is true with the warmth of the sun. Tell a man who has no feeling that it is a warm day and he will never understand what you mean. But take a normal man who is out in the warm sun and he will soon know it is warm. You can know more about the sun by feeling than you can by description.

So there are qualities in God that can never be explained to the intellect and can only be known by the heart, the innermost being. That is why I say that I do believe in feeling. I believe in what the old writers called religious affection—and we have so little of it because we have not laid the groundwork for it. The groundwork is repentance and obedience and separation and holy living!

I am confident that whenever this groundwork is laid, there will come to us this sense of the other-worldly Presence of God and it will become wonderfully, wonderfully real.

I have at times heard an expression in our prayers, "Oh, God, draw feelingly near!"

I don't think that God is too far off—in spite of those who can only draw back and sit in judgment.

"Oh, God, come feelingly near!" God drew feelingly near to Moses in the bush and on the mount. He came feelingly near to the church at Pentecost and He came feelingly near to that Corinthian church when the unbelievers went away awe-struck to report that "God is really in their midst!"

I am willing to confess in humility that we need this in our day.

God Names Me
His Beneficiary!

*. . . into an inheritance that can never
perish, spoil or fade.* (1 Peter 1:4)

I'm a rich man—God Himself has named me
His beneficiary!

I came to the conclusion long ago that a
Christian who places a proper value upon the
true riches of eternity will have little inclination
to fret and worry about being remembered
here in some relative's last will and testament.

Peter deals with this matter of the reality of
the divine benefits, describing our future inheritance with the words "that can never
perish, spoil or fade."

He indicates that those persecuted and down-
trodden strangers in the early church were
believers in Jesus Christ, elect and begotten.
The electing and the begetting were means
leading into a hope and an inheritance, but
they were not the end.

We would all be better Christians and wiser students if we would remember this—God rarely uses periods. There is rarely a full stop in His dealings with us—it is more likely to be with the effect of a colon or a semi-colon. In most instances, what God does becomes a means toward something else that He is planning to do.

Therefore, when God elects a man it does not mean that the man can sit down at his ease and announce, "I have arrived," because the election is only unto a begetting. Can any man who is begotten of the Spirit and has become a Christian believer presume to say, "I have arrived! Put a period there and write finis across my experience"?

No, of course not. God begets us into His provision and that which is still before us is always bigger than that which is behind us. This is certainly true of His provision for us in the divine inheritance.

We ought to get the facts straight

Now, I think we ought to get the facts straight. Peter was not merely using a figure of speech when he insisted that the begotten one, the true Christian believer, is actually the beneficiary of God. This is not a figure. It is not just a poetic phrase and neither is it an isolated reference. It is openly taught from Genesis to Revelation that the true believer stands to benefit from an inheritance. God being who He is, His beneficence and His benefits are infinite and limitless.

I believe that God always touches with infinity everything that He does and this leads to the thought that the inheritance we receive must be equal to the God who gives it. Being God, He does not deal in things which are merely finite. Therefore, the inheritance that the child of God receives is limitless and infinite.

What a contrast to our small gifts and legacies and benefits on this earth!

I recall that my father used to drive along the way and point to some great farm area and comment: "I hope before I die that I can buy that and leave it to you." But he didn't leave very much. I signed a quit-claim to one little piece of property and hurried it back airmail special.

We do benefit from our parents, however. They give us certain physical and mental inheritances. But they cannot give us what they do not have and it is always limited on this earth. Even the world's richest man can only leave what he has—nothing more. Somewhere, the millions give out and every estate has a boundary.

But, God being who He is, the inheritance we receive from Him is limitless—it is all of the universe!

That is the reason why no hymn writer has ever been able to state the facts, all of the facts, about God's eternal provision for His children. They can only sketch it. It is rather like gathering sea shells on the shores of the vast ocean that stretches away with island upon island, continent upon continent, all belonging to God and to His people in redemption. It all comes from Him!

The infinite benefactions of God

We humans should remember that when our high flights of imagination have taken wings upward we can be sure that we have never quite reached as high as His provision, because our imagination will always falter, run out of energy and fall weakly to the ground. In contrast, there is no limit to the infinite benefactions of God Almighty to His redeemed ones.

Brethren, the Christian believer stands to receive riches for all parts of his being.

We are physical and mental and moral and spiritual—and I suppose we may say social. We are all of these.

Some Christians do not like the word *social* because they think it means going to church and eating out of a box, like a church social. But we are social in our being. We do have relationships—with the neighbors, in our precinct, to our state, our country and, in a larger way, to the whole world.

I have always thought that Bernard of Cluny, writing about 1140 A.D., knew what he was talking about when he said:

I know not, Oh, I know not
What social joys are there;
What radiancy of glory,
What joy beyond compare.

He says there are social joys in heaven and I
think it is perfectly true.

But man also has a spiritual life and a moral
life, a mental life and a physical life. He may
also have hidden facets of his life that are not
thus classified for we are more than mental or
physical beings. We are more than moral, although morality ought to touch all the rest of
our being.

And, we are more than spiritual beings, although if we were not spiritual beings, we
would not be much better than the beasts.

The point I make is this: we stand to receive
infinite benefits from God in all parts of our nature. I refer, of course, to Christian believers,
the promises having been made to the
redeemed. The sinner, the alien from God, has
no moral right even to get old, to say nothing
of dying, because the older he gets the nearer
he moves toward the grave and judgment and
hell.

But the redeemed and believing child of God
can afford to get sick and to get old. He even
has a right to die—for God has made provision
for a new body and for the mental life, the
moral life and the spiritual life—a provision
which is actually unsearchable.

The word unsearchable

I like that word *unsearchable*. It is a good word. I am reminded that Clarence Darrow thought he was inferring something nasty when he insisted that Christians always say "It is a mystery" when there is some aspect of Christian faith or truth that defies description.

I have never accepted it as a nasty remark. I take it in a friendly way because the Christian does run into mystery almost everywhere he looks. The difference between the believer and the worldling is that the world is always running into mystery and calling it science or some such thing, while we are frank to admit that we don't know what it is. I admit that I do not know the full implications of the word *unsearchable*.

We get a hint when we talk about the unsearchable riches of Christ—riches that cannot be counted or measured, riches that cannot be fully searched out. These are riches that have so many glorious ramifications and endless qualities that their value cannot be comprehended.

They are the unsearchable riches of Christ and because God is the Living God and the Christian stands in the relationship of child of God, he has the promise of the divine inheritance—the riches which cannot be fully searched out.

Now, God's benefactions are dispensed in

three ways and if you will really consider these, you will be helped when you think and pray and read your Bible!

First, I believe God is busy giving us direct, present benefactions.

There are some things which God gives directly in this present age while we are still on our feet, still alive, still conscious, still in this vale of tears and laughter.

For instance, He gives forgiveness. He is pleased to bestow forgiveness upon His believing children.

He gives eternal life. This is not an inheritance to be received at some time in the future; our life in Him is a present bestowment. It is now a present gift which we have. The forgiven sinner has this life the moment he believes.

God also gives us sonship: "Dear friends, now are we children of God" (1 John 3:2a). In this relationship there are many other gifts we receive from God—and if we do not possess them it is because we are not God's children by faith.

Countless other gifts

Perhaps I should also speak of countless other gifts. We ask God to help us, and the Lord mercifully does it. I consider these the little and the trifling things, yet we make a great deal of them. But they are really the passing things compared to the great present benefactions of forgiveness, reinstatement in favor with God, sonship and eternal life.

Then, God has a second way of dispensing His blessings and that is by giving them as a reward for loving and faithful service in His name. The Bible portrays this truth—that some of the riches of God may come in the nature of a reward.

We are aware that all things belong to God, all riches and all blessings, and even though we talk about earning a reward, that is not really a proper expression. There isn't any sense in which we humans can earn God's benefactions.

Actually, as loving and faithful children of God, we are meeting a condition whereby God can bestow blessing as a reward for meeting that condition. That's about all there is to it.

He has said, "Well done, good and faithful servant! You have been faithful with a few things; I will put you in charge of many things" (Matthew 25:21a). He has spoken of his rewards with the admonition: "Be faithful even to the point of death, and I will give you the crown of life" (Revelation 2:10b). These are things that God will bestow as the result of faithful and loyal service and they are future rewards, not yet to be received.

The third manner of God's bestowment is by way of inheritance. The blessings and riches of our divine inheritance are also to be realized in the future. These are not riches that will come to us for anything that is worthy or superior in ourselves, but because of our relationship in faith to the One who is the fount of every blessing.

He delights to honor

In this inheritance the riches come from One who possesses and owns all to another whom He delights to honor and who can establish his rightful claim. This is a principle that we know well in our probate courts—this is why we have recorded wills and bequests. These must all go through the probate court process and those who are named in the wills must establish their identification and rights to the inheritance through relationship.

Now, I repeat—an inheritance has not actually been earned. A boy may be very much of an ingrate and still prove his right to an inheritance because his father delighted to honor him and, because he was his son, made him his sole heir. The will is written and witnessed and on record so when the father dies it is only a matter of going before the proper authorities and proving identity and relationship as the rightful son. It is the right resulting from a relationship—not necessarily the right of goodness. So, there is an inheritance that belongs to the children of God by virtue of the fact that they are truly children of God.

But here I want you to note how many earthly things are upside down in contrast to that of the heavenly.

Among men, a legacy is received at the time of the death of the one who gives the legacy, the testator. But in the things of God, the legacy comes upon the death of the legatee, that is, the person who inherits.

That all sounds confused enough without my confusing it more, but I will try to put it in the form of another illustration.

Suppose a man has a son, an only son. He executes his will making his son the sole heir and giving him everything in the estate. But as long as the father lives that will does not become operative for the son as heir.

But, one day the father is stricken and dies.

After the proper period of mourning, the son goes before the probate authorities and proves that he is the one who is to receive the inheritance. He comes into possession of the inherited estate because his father had died and the will has become operative on behalf of the son.

In the kingdom of God, it is exactly opposite—just the other way around!

The Father promises and provides an inheritance to His children, but this inheritance is not to be validated by the death of God, but actually upon the death of the child of God or at the coming of Christ, which adds up to the same thing in terms of the inheritance.

Paul knew about the inheritance and he expected it. He wrote about the fact that believers are co-heirs with Christ. He declares that we will realize this in its full implications when we see Christ face to face in a future time. I have said that only a Christian has the right and can afford to die. But if we believers were as spiritual as we ought to be, we might be looking forward to death with a great deal more pleasure and anticipation than we do!

Anticipate the second advent

I say that if we are truly believers in the second advent of the Savior, we will be anticipating that second advent. Common sense and the perspective of history, the testimony of the saints, reason and the Bible all agree with one voice that He may come before you die.

Nevertheless, "it is appointed unto man once to die" (Hebrews 9:27, KJV)—and the Christian knows that he may die before the Lord comes. If he dies, he is better off, for Paul said, "I desire to depart and be with Christ, which is better by far" (Philippians 1:23b).

The difference between a believer living on this earth or being promoted into the presence of Christ is the difference between "good" and "better," according to Paul.

Now, in conclusion, the Christian's future is still before him. I will give you time to smile at that, because it sounds like a self-evident bromide if ever one was uttered. But I assure that it is not a self-evident banality; it is rather a proof that we ought to ponder soberly the fact that many Christians already have their fu-

ture behind them. Their glory is behind them.
The only future they have is their past. They
are always lingering around the cold ashes of
yesterday's burned-out campfire. Their testimonies indicate it, their outlook and their
uplook reveal it and their downcast look
betrays it! I always get an uneasy feeling when
I find myself with people who have nothing to
discuss but the glories of the days that are past.

Yes, the Christian's future is before him. The
whole direction of the Christian's look should
be forward.

Always looking forward

Paul was an example for us in this regard for
in his soul and spirit he was always looking
forward. In his writing we find that he looked
back only very briefly and I take it as we read
that it is perfectly proper to occasionally steal a
quick, happy backward look to see where we
have been and to remind ourselves of the grace
and goodness of God to us and to our fellow
believers.

There is a small word from the Latin—*spect*—
which has different forms and it means to see
or to look. In our English, that little word has
two prefixes which can be used. They are *retro*,
meaning backward, and *pro*, meaning forward.

Do you know that the richness of your Christian life, your usefulness and your fruitfulness,
depend upon which prefix you attach to that
word? You are bound to be looking some-

where! Even if you are blind, you are looking somewhere for your soul has to dwell either on the past or on the future. Your soul is facing in some direction as a Christian and the Bible advises us to look steadfastly unto Jesus, the Author and Finisher of our faith.

We are either retrospective or prospective in our outlook and our whole future depends in great measure upon which way we look. In that, I mean our future here on earth and perhaps even our future in the world to come.

We ought not emphasize the "retrospective." Let us speak of the past only when we have to. Paul wrote, "Forgetting what is behind . . . I press on!" (Philippians 3:13–14a). There were only a few times when he had to do it, but he stood and pointed back and told of his conversion—and that's legitimate!

But it is my advice that we ought not to get locked into that position of looking back. Why should you get a sore neck from looking back over your own shoulder?

Personally, I have found that God will take care of that fellow behind me, even if I can feel him breathing on my neck.

Prospect is the word for you and me. Look forward! Look ahead! Live with faith and expectation because the Christian's future is more glorious than his past!

One moment of the Christian's tomorrow will be more wonderful than all the glories of his yesterdays. Methuselah lived 969 years on earth and yet if he died and went to be with God, and I think he did, one single hour in the presence of God was more wonderful to him than any part of his 969 years on this earth!

So, Christians, let us look forward! Look forward with expectation and hope because we are begotten again unto an inheritance and that inheritance comes from God our Father and is ours by virtue of our relationship to Him in faith.

Yes, we do have the benefits of present gifts and there are things which will be considered rewards; but the inheritance is ours because we are children of God!

That means that we have every reason to cheer up, believing and hoping, and looking forward to that day of God. For the most eloquent tongue or the most exquisite poetry can never adequately paint for us the glories that we will possess eternally by inheritance, by virtue of our sonship to God and our gracious relationship to Christ, our Savior!

Qualities of a Divine Inheritance!

*. . . an inheritance that can never
perish, spoil or fade—kept
in heaven for you.*
(1 Peter 1:4)

The corrosive action of unbelief in our day has worn down the Christian hope of heaven until there seems to be very little joy and expectation concerning the eternal inheritance which God has promised.

I think we have a right to be startled by the thought that very few people really believe in heaven any more. Oh, we may hear a hillbilly with a guitar singing about heaven in a way that would make an intelligent man turn away from the thought of such a heaven. But, for the most part, we do not think about heaven very often and we talk about it even less!

Two men in our human history have had great influence upon modern man's general thinking in regard to heaven and the universe. I refer to Copernicus and Einstein.

Geocentric thinking

Before Copernicus, men were geocentric in their thinking. They considered the earth to be everything and the center of everything. This was largely man's concept—"God made the earth and put it here and everything revolves around it. It is solid and fixed. God has nailed it down and established the foundations and there is nothing that can change that."

But along came Copernicus and, willing to risk his life as a heretic, proved that the earth does not stand still and it is not nailed down. As an astronomer he insisted that the sun, not the earth, is the center of the universe and the sun only seems to stand in the earth's motion. The sun, in fact, moves in a wider orbit, a faster and all but limitless orbit out yonder through the vast, vast space.

So that knowledge filtered down from the scientists into the colleges and then into the high schools and from the grade schools onto the street. Everyone knows it and accepts it now, with this common question resulting: "What about this heaven idea?"

There was a day when heaven was right "up there" and the stars were its peepholes. You could look up and see a bit of the light of the glory that was never on land or sea.

But now, the idea that heaven is actually a

place is something to laugh about, for men have allowed new ideas and information about the universe to act like a corrosive in wearing down their belief in heaven.

The second man to whom I refer was Einstein who came along with his theories and statements of relativity. He not only took out the earth but he took out the sun and the stars and everything, insisting that nothing is actually fixed or established anywhere. It was his theory that nothing is standing still—everything is in motion. Everything exists only in relation to something else. There is not one thing against which you can measure something else and conclude, "That's it!" This can go on ad infinitum, world without end, and there is nothing absolutely fixed, according to Einstein.

I do not know about you, but I get to a certain point with the theories of scholarship where I am inclined to say: "Oh, rest my long-divided heart, fixed on this blissful center, rest!"

There is a place where neither Copernicus nor Einstein troubleth and I am able to rest in the wisdom and love of God, who made all of these whirling planets and the worlds which are within the worlds!

Science should not erode faith in heaven

Personally, I do not see why the idea of relativity or the motions of the heavenly bodies should destroy or erode the Christian's faith in heaven as a place. If God could create an earth and put a race on it, why could He not create another home and put a redeemed race on it?

Perhaps it can be attributed to my small mind and untroubled intellect, but I do not have the problem that some people have in giving God that much credit—that if He would make the earth a race of humans, He could surely make another place and call it heaven and put on it a race that has been redeemed. This is very simple for me!

So Copernicus and Einstein can lie down with their follies and they won't bother me at all. But I do realize they have taken away the idea and reality of heaven from many people.

Some are saying, "Heaven is just another dimension, let's not try to figure it out." Still others say that heaven is a state of mind having to do entirely with life here upon the earth.

All of our human reasoning which does not take the Word of God into account is simply the artful dodging of unbelief. I still believe that the God who made earth and put people here can make heaven to be the habitation of His redeemed people. Do you?

Incorruptible, undefiled and unfading

Perhaps in our churches we have not adequately taught the qualities of the divine inheritance which awaits the children of God. Let us look now at three words used by Peter to describe the qualities of our heavenly inheritance and note that they are precisely the qualities that belong to our heavenly inheritance through Christ Jesus our Lord.

These are the words he uses: *incorruptible, undefiled* and *unfading*. These are the inherent qualities of our heavenly legacy. These are part of it and they describe it. They do not define it, but they are the qualities that belong to our heavenly inheritance through Christ Jesus our Lord.

I think we must come to this point in our faith concerning God's great future plans for His children: to believe that the things of God and heaven are not simply an upward projection of our imagination of the very best that we have or can know or can imagine in this world. Actually, they are contrary to the things of earth because of their heavenly qualities—incorruptible, undefiled and unfading!

According to the meaning in the Greek language, our word *incorruptible* expresses the quality of undecaying in essence and endless in years. That which cannot be corrupted is undecaying in essence and, I suppose, only secondarily endless in years.

I ask you if there is anything on this earth that can properly and accurately be described as incorruptible, that does not decay in its essence and is endless in its sphere?

Our Lord Jesus said, "Do not store up for yourselves treasures on earth, where moth and rust destroy, and where thieves break in and steal" (Matthew 6:19). Now, those were not the words of a defeatist.

I know that we Christians are often charged with being defeatists. Psychologists will tell you that the black man in the South sings so beautifully about heaven and the golden streets because he has owned only a wooden shack. Therefore, in his mind he is trying to create for himself what his master possessed in the slave days, and that is his idea of heaven.

Similarly, they tell us now that heaven is the dream of those who are defeated and unhappy—a dream of a happy, happy land where no one needs to wipe away a tear.

Well, that would explain everything except for the small matter that it is not true. Our Lord Jesus Christ was not a defeatist. He did not suffer as they said Abraham suffered. Because Lincoln pitied people, the experts surmise that he suffered from a "glandular deficiency."

Not a defeatist

Our Lord Jesus Christ had no such deficiency and He was not a defeatist. On the other hand, He certainly was not a silly optimist. Neither did He have any of the gloomy, heavy-hearted pessimism that has characterized a great many of this world's thinkers.

Jesus saw everything clearly and in a true light! If there ever existed in the wide world a man who earned the right to be called a realist, Jesus Christ was that man.

It was all real to Him. He never shaded one edge of anything to bring something else into relief. He saw everything exactly as it was and described it and spoke of it exactly as it was.

Jesus Christ was the world's most perfect realist because He Himself was Truth!

Therefore, He was neither dreaming of some heaven that He had never seen, nor was He projecting His imagination upward away from the grief and miseries of this world to some lovely heaven, some mansion which was being prepared.

He spoke of things as they were and as they will be found to be. He spoke of all of man's treasures and warned that moth and rust will corrupt. He said corruption is an earthly reality and it is futile for a man to put his trust in the vanity of the corruptible things which he may possess.

Oh, what a cheat the devil is! What a deceiver and what a confidence man he is!

I think of the cheating devil when I think of the sly confidence men who have sold the Brooklyn Bridge to poor people, grinning as they have taken their last dollar, leaving them to find out too late that the Brooklyn Bridge was never on the market.

The devil is a liar, I say, and a deceiver. He is busy leading people to spend the best years of their lives laying up treasures for themselves, which even before they die will begin to rust and rot and decay.

Incorruptible is a word that cannot be applied to any earthly thing. There is nothing that we can know down here that is undecaying in its essence and endless in its years. But there is an inheritance which Jesus Christ the realist, Jesus Christ the heavenly one, came to give to His believing saints.

The resurrection

All of this leads on to the resurrection. This word *incorruptible* used to describe a quality of our inheritance is the very same word describing the state of the dead who are to rise up at the coming of Jesus Christ.

In one of our great Christian anthems, the singers declare with great feeling: "The dead shall be raised incorruptible!" That is exactly the same word describing the glorified human body that Peter used to describe the heavenly inheritance of the saints.

It cannot decay. It cannot be corrupted.

As a human being, I must think of what Job said in the Old Testament about the human prospect. Weary, sick and tired, Job said that he knew that the skin worms would devour his body. In spite of the fact that I like to spend my time thinking along more pleasant lines, I am well aware that the forces and elements that will devour our bodies in the grave are already at work in our physical bodies.

But God Himself has promised that there will be a day when those worms will be no more.

God will shake them loose and He will say:
"Let him alone. Let him alone forever!" The
Bible says that the children of God will be
raised with incorruptible bodies.

Incorruptible—without decay and endless in
years! That is why I have said that this quality
describing our heavenly inheritance is precisely
the quality that distinguishes it from all earthly
things.

The second quality

For the second quality of our inheritance,
Peter uses the word *undefiled*.

The question we must ask ourselves immediately is this: What earthly treasure do any of us
possess that is safe from defilement?

The Bible has very few kind things to say
about money and earthly possessions and it is
most frank in its expressions against the heap-
ing up of treasures.

The Bible mentions lucre, describing money
and profit and earthly gain, and then drops in a
startling and descriptive adjective to make it
"filthy lucre."

The Apostle Paul, who was not a defeatist
and was not compelled to rationalize his
poverty, had given up a prominent position to
become a follower of Jesus Christ. He wrote
that the love of money is a root from which evil
springs. He did not single out money itself, but
he spoke of an attitude and condition of a
man's heart that could put his greed and self-

ishness and love of money above everything else. We should note, too, that Paul did not insist that all evil springs from the love of money, but said that love of money is one of the roots from which evil springs.

Now, money and every other thing that we have in this world are defiled and have been defiled. A saint of God may own and possess certain things, but they rarely come to him without having been defiled.

You may have a ten-dollar bill folded in your wallet which you intend to give to the missionary cause. There is always a possibility that those dollars were once a part of a wad paid to someone to commit a murder. Or, it could easily have been part of a purse of money handed out in a gambling den or a scandalous brothel.

It has always seemed to me that the very smell of the currency we pass around indicates where it has been. It smells like itself—as though it could tell its own story of crime and violence and immorality!

Must keep ourselves clean

Brethren, we keep ourselves clean in the midst of human defilement because we know the cleansing power of the blood of Christ, our Savior! It is not morally wrong for us to have money for our needs, but we ought to guard our own spirits against defilement by virtue of the washing of the blood of Christ.

There is an element of defilement upon

everything in this lost world. The very lot upon which your house now stands once belonged to an Indian tribe, and history is very plain in recounting the sad story. We white men came and without any payment in kind kicked the Indians out to the western sea. We put them on little lice-infested reservations and tossed them a pittance from year to year, trying to salve our consciences!

On the other hand, historians and anthropologists also tell us that the Indians we abused and chased out had in a previous time invaded the land and taken it from a race that preceded them.

It is the same situation around the world. Go to the map of Europe and you will see how men have argued and fought for their borders, those flexible and changing borders.

Long ago I threw up my hands in confusion and said, "I will never be able to decide which nation owns what land over there." If we go back far enough in history, we will find those who have the land got it by invasion, by massacre, by murder. Then they had squatters' rights, forgetting how they seized it with the only payment being the blood of the people that owned it.

Almost everything is defiled

So, almost everything we touch in this life is defiled. Injustice and oppression run through everything. You know what I think about the devil-possessed origins of communism and its godless partisans who criticize our faith and our ideals and our way of life. But it is the human defilement on every hand which gives the communist his one lone weapon—because what he says about us is not all lies.

I am pained by the injustices in our society. I drive by the gleaming mansions and the stately lake shore hotels—and what do I think about?

I think about the poor, tired old women with their buckets and mops. Weary, often-defeated and disenchanted people—thankful for a small wage for a night's dreary work!

Drive down the coast of Florida and notice those graceful yachts floating at anchor. It is our natural inclination to think: "It must be fantastic to be in that bracket!"

But if you knew how much of iniquity there was wrought into one of those graceful things, you would never desire it for yourself!

Not a political comment

Emerson once said to a young man with political aspirations: "Young man, you want to be president? You want to go to the White House? Ah, if you only knew how much of his manhood that man had to sell out to get there, you wouldn't want it. If you only knew how he must obey those who stand erect behind the throne and tell him what to do, you wouldn't want it!"

I do not make this as a political comment. No

matter which party is in office or what man is in office, it is true that everything is defiled all over the world.

Why? Because everything flows out of the human being and the human being is defiled. You cannot draw pure water from a defiled fountain. You cannot pluck sweet figs from a thorn tree. You cannot pick sweet grapes from a wild vine and you certainly cannot get edible chicken eggs from a buzzard.

Likewise, you cannot get pure treasures from impure hearts!

Before we leave this subject, I must make this observation: I do not go along with those who hold that every businessman is a crook. I want to say that I know there are men in public life who would scornfully turn their back on anything that is not honest and fair. I believe, particularly in the Christian faith, that it is possible to live a clean and upright life.

My point is this: because of humanity's lost and defiled condition, money and influence and power generally bear the taint and touch of defilement on them. This is in contrast to the believer's divine inheritance, pure and unsoiled.

So, we trace our inheritance back to its source. Because it flowed out of the pure, undefiled heart of Jesus Christ, it is as undefiled as He is, and He is the one who is described as holy and harmless and undefiled, separate from sinners.

It is unfading

The third quality of our eternal inheritance is that it fadeth not away. It is unfading!

Now, I refer you to your knowledge of this present world once again. Do you know of anything in this present world that can be described as unfading in quality or value?

In all of our larger cities, you can drive down certain streets and avenues and find clusters of old brownstone mansions. When they were built, they were the pride of the wealthy and the elite. They were a mark of social standing and of the so-called "blue bloods."

But the years have passed and the splendor of those mansions has faded away. In many places they are now shabby and in need of repair, often housing a dozen or more families of low income status.

The social royalty of a few generations ago has passed away. Though their names were in the Who's Who they didn't happen to know what's what! In their lifetime they would not have dreamed that those mansions would deteriorate, lose their value and, in effect, fade away.

That is the way it is with the things of this life.

A young man marries his bride today in her blushing womanhood. She is beautiful to behold. But a few years pass and she notices this human process that we call fading.

So, she scrambles off to the beauty parlor and the cosmetics counter and probably even to the pharmacist in the drug store; she feels she has to do something to prop up her fading beauty.

Also, I know lots of men who may not be concerned about their looks but they are supporting the druggists and the medicine houses because of an ulcer or a rheumatic pain; they realize their physical health is fading!

Old letters fade as do old books and other old things. Sometimes they can be restored for a price, but in another generation or two they will have to be restored again and each restoration means a fading.

The Bible plainly and clearly tells us that we are like the flower of the field that fadeth. Today it is and tomorrow it is cut down and is withered and gone.

I don't mind telling you that I am vitally interested in this inheritance which is reserved in heaven for us! As far as I am concerned, it is just as real as my right hand. I am satisfied with Peter's description of our future inheritance and his promise that we are kept by the power of God through faith unto that inheritance.

"Kept by the power of God through faith unto an inheritance . . . "

Why does Peter speak of us in this way? Why didn't he speak of the inheritance itself as being kept?

No, he speaks of our inheritance and then

plainly says, "We are kept by the power of God."

The answer

I think I have the answer.

It would be unthinkable if our inheritance was incorruptible and then we corrupted, wouldn't it?

It would be unthinkable if our inheritance was unfading and we ourselves faded.

It would be unthinkable if our treasure outlasted us and God found Himself in the embarrassing position of preparing unfading treasure for a people He could not keep to enjoy it!

Is God going to be caught in such an emotional tangle? Is God going to allow Himself to preserve an inheritance for a people whom He cannot preserve?

Never, never! Not while the world stands, for we are kept by the power of God through faith unto an inheritance reserved in heaven for us.

So, I am leaning back very strongly on the keeping power of God!

Now, finally, if you are being kept by the power of God, what kind of indications of that plan and of that power are being reflected in your daily life?

Peter has made it plain in this same passage: we are elect, begotten, obedient and believing!

That is the entire answer.

Elect—that is God's business and it was His business before we knew anything about it!

Begotten—that is God's business as we believe in His Son!

Obedient and believing—we who are kept by the power of God through faith unto an inheritance.

So there we are, friends—and as Christians, we are not only rich but nobly rich! Rich with riches which need no apology. Riches which have no taint of having come to us through defiled hands!

I wonder when we will begin to behave and to live on the level of our riches instead of acting like poverty-stricken creatures trying to crawl under a leaf so we will not be seen.

Let's let the world know how rich we really are! Let's tell it—we are being kept by the power of God unto an inheritance reserved in heaven for us!

That's the full-time business of the child of God!

Was Your Humility
Showing Today?

*All of you, clothe yoursleves with
humility . . . because "God opposes the
proud but gives grace to the humble."*
(1 Peter 5:5)

The Apostle Peter, advising Christian
believers to be clothed with humility in all
of their relationships with one another, actually
infers that genuine Christian humility should
be their identifying uniform from day to day!

In the custom of that distant culture, men
dressed according to their status and place in
society.

In our own day, we also are accustomed to
identifying many public servants by the kind of
uniform they wear. If we suddenly need help
or assistance, even in a strange city, we look
around quickly to find a helpful man in the
policeman's uniform.

We have no fear of the mailman who daily

steps on our property. His gray uniform tells us that he is a servant of our government and that he has a responsibility for helpful public service.

So, the Holy Spirit through the apostle cites the necessity for members of the Body of Christ to be subject to one another in the bonds of love, mercy and grace. This honest posture of submission and humility becomes our uniform, and adornment really, indicating that we are the redeemed and obedient disciples of Jesus Christ and that we belong to Him!

Peter's request is not strange when we remember that it was Jesus Christ our Lord who dressed himself in humility and then took that difficult course down, down, down—to the death on the cross!

It is a scriptural and divine example that we have in the person of Jesus,

> Who, being in very nature God,
>   did not consider equality with God
>   something to be grasped,
> But made himself nothing,
>   taking the very nature of a servant,
>   being made in human likeness.
> And being found in appearance as a man,
>   he humbled himself
>   and became obedient to death—even
>   death on a cross!
> Therefore God exalted him to the highest
>   place

and gave him the name that is above
every name. (Philippians 2:6–9)

I think it is most important for believers to ac-
knowledge the fact that because Christ Jesus
came to the world clothed in humility, He will
always be found among those who are clothed
with humility. He will be found among the
humble people. This is a lesson that not all of
us have learned.

I want to refer here to a rather striking passage in the Song of Songs which I think throws
practical light upon the desire of the heavenly
Bridegroom to be in fellowship with those dear
to him in places of humble service.

I am using this Old Testament story as a good
and forceful illustration even though someone
may insist that it does not stand up under the
rigorous criticism of the Bible scholar and ex-
positor. Frankly I do not know how anyone is
going to soundly expound the Song of Songs—
we are more likely to get every man's idea of
what it means!

The illustration is in chapter five and the
bride is telling of her distress because her
beloved had called her during the evening to
go with him and she was slow to respond. He
called to her saying that his head was covered
with the dew and his locks with the drops of
the night, for he had been gathering lilies and
myrrh and caring for his sheep.

In a kind of summary, she recalls that she

was garbed beautifully for the night chamber but not in the attire which would allow her to respond quickly to his call, for he wanted her to join him in his humility and service among the sheep and in the duties of the gardens and fields.

Then she confesses: "I opened for my lover, but my love had left; he was gone. . . . I looked for him but I did not find him. I called him but he did not answer" (5:6).

By the time she was willing to put on the proper garment to join him in his humble duties, he was gone.

Now, the Scriptures are conclusive in teaching that God is always on the side of the humble man and Peter is in full agreement with the statement that God resists the proud and gives grace to the humble.

Perhaps human beings are generally of the opinion that they will find Jesus Christ wherever they are; but I think there is such a thing as finding Christ wherever He is—and that will be in the place of humility, always!

Resisting pride

God resists the man who is proud—and stubborn! I believe God has to consider the attitude of the proud man as being resistance to Him. It is not very often—perhaps once in a hundred years—that a person will actually raise his face to God and exclaim: "God, I resist you; I defy you!"

There is no general pattern of that kind of defiance among men. We are much more likely to oppose God by resisting the side He is on and resisting His ways.

But the Scriptures plainly teach that when a proud and stubborn man resists God, he may expect to find that God is resisting him.

The man who sets his jaw and takes action against a Christian, even though he may be right in point of fact, nevertheless will find God in resistance to him because he is wrong in spirit and attitude.

God looks to spirit and attitude

I think God looks beyond the situation to the spirit and attitude. I think He is more concerned with how we react to abuse and mistreatment than to the fact that we have been abused by someone.

Some of us have had experiences of being "told off" most eloquently by people with a very descriptive flow of language; but the eloquence is lost completely insofar as God is concerned. If you are His child taking some abuse or persecution for His sake, His great concern is the attitude that you will show in return.

Will you reveal a stubborn spirit intent upon revenge? If you resist the Spirit of God asking you to demonstrate the love and grace of Jesus Christ, your Savior, you can be sure of one thing: God will resist you!

Now, that doesn't mean that God is going to

switch and take the side of the other man who has abused you. It just means that God will have to resist you because He will always resist the stubborn man.

Even if you have the facts on your side, God will know whether you are wrong in your spirit. When God resists a man for his pride, it is not likely that He will send immediate and dramatic judgment. God probably will not signal His resistance to the stubborn man by a judgment that will come in the public place.

Rarely does God send His judgment dramatically. I have wondered if we might learn our lessons of humility and obedience more quickly if God were to resist a man as one soldier to another, with the clash of sword and the letting of blood?

Inward spiritual degeneration

But it does not work that way. When God resists a man for the sins of his spirit and attitude, a slow, inward spiritual degeneration will take place as a signal of the judgment that has come. A slow hardening that comes from unwillingness to yield will result in cynicism. The Christian joy will disappear and there will be no more fruits of the Spirit. That man will sour as a jar of fruit sours—and it is not an exaggeration to say that the man who has earned the resistance of God will continue to sour bitterly in his own juice.

God does resist the proud and I think the significant factor is this: the man may not have been wrong in point of fact, but he failed the test in his spirit!

Grace for the humble

It is significant, too, that the Scripture assures us that the same God who must resist the proud always stands ready to give grace to the humble. The Bible advises men and women to humble themselves under the mighty hand of God. It is my opinion that if our humility had to show itself only under the hand of God, it would be a relatively easy gesture.

If the Lord should say to me, "I am coming and will stand at the front of the church and I will expect you to come and kneel before me and humble yourself," it would be an easy thing for me to do because I know that no one will ever lose face in kneeling humbly before God Himself.

Any man would feel just as proud as ever even though kneeling before the eternal Majesty on high. But God knows our hearts and He doesn't allow us to fulfill His demands for humility with a mere gesture.

God may use people whom you think are not worthy to shine your shoes and in a given situation He will expect you to humble yourself meekly and take from them whatever it is they are pouring on you. In that spirit of meekness you would be humbling yourself under the mighty hand of God!

Think of the example of our Savior, cruelly beaten and cut with the lash. That whip was not wielded by an archangel but by the hands of a pagan Roman soldier. The abuse that was heaped on Jesus did not come from any multitude of the heavenly host—but from wicked, blasphemous and dirty-tongued men who were not worthy to clean the dust from the soles of His sandals.

Jesus willingly humbled Himself under the hand of men and so He humbled Himself under the hand of God.

Christians have often asked: "Must I humble myself and meekly accept every situation in life?"

Humility must never violate truth

I think this is the answer: As Christians, we must never violate morals or truth in humility.

If in humbling ourselves we compromise the truth, we must never do it. If it means a compromise of morality, we must never do it.

I am confident that no man is ever called of God to degrade himself, either morally or in truth. But we do have calling from God to humble ourselves under His mighty hand—and let the other party do the rock-throwing!

In this call to His people for true humility, God adds the promise that He will exalt us in due time! "Due time." I think that means a time that is proper to all of the circumstances. It will be the time that God knows is best suited to perfect us and a time that will bring honor to God and the most good to men. That is "due time."

It may be that in God's will He will expect us to wait a long time before He can honor us or exalt us. He may let us labor in humility and subjection for a long period because it is not yet His time—due time.

Brethren, God knows what is best for each of us in His desire to make us the kind of saints that will glorify and honor Him in all things!

Many of us have harmed our own children in such ways as these: teaching them to drive our cars before they were old enough; giving them too much freedom before they knew the meaning of responsibility and maturity.

These things come out of our misdirected kindnesses, but they will harm the child. To reward a man for things he has not earned and does not deserve will surely harm the man.

Saints must go through fire

Likewise, for God to come too quickly to the defense, before the saint has gone through the fire, will harm the saint.

We are faced here with Bible truth and not with the fiction of men.

A modern book of fiction would have had Daniel well protected. As he was about to be placed in the lions' den, a voice out of the sky would have spoken and every lion would have dropped dead.

But what actually happened?

God allowed Daniel's enemies to put him in the den of lions and he slept there with the lions until morning because God's "due time" for Daniel was in the morning, not the night before!

I would also like to see how the modern fiction writers would handle the story of the three Hebrew children in the fiery furnace. They could make a whole book out of that!

They would be forced to some climactic, human trick to put out that fire just before the three young men were to be tossed into the furnace—but that would be putting out the fire too soon!

For God to have His own way and to be glorified in due time, those saints had to go into the fire and stay there throughout the night—due time was in the morning.

God's time

God has said He will exalt you in due time, but remember, He is referring to His time and not yours!

Some of you are actually in a fiery furnace right now. You are in a special kind of spiritual testing. The pastor may not know it and others may not know it, but you have been praying and asking the Lord: "Why don't you get me out of this?"

In God's plan it is not yet "due time." When you have come through the fire, God will get you out and there will not be any smell of smoke on your garment and you will not have been harmed.

The only harm that can come will be from your insistence that God must get you out sooner than He plans.

The Lord has promised to exalt you in due time and He has always kept His promises to His people.

As children of God, we can always afford to wait. A saint of God does not have to be concerned about time when he is in the will of God.

It is the sinner who has no time. He has to hurry or he will go to hell, but the Christian has an eternity of blessedness before him.

Wait it out

So, if you are in a furnace, don't try to come out too soon! Wait it out in the will of God and He will exalt you in due time—time proper to the circumstances. It will be a time properly designed to glorify God and to bless your own spirit!

One of our great weaknesses as Christian men and women is our continued insistence upon getting vindicated before the trial is over. God has said that He wants to try us and test us and when the trial is over, He Himself will bring in the verdict: "Tested—and found worthy!"

I only pray that we all may know how to conduct ourselves as trusting children of God during this period in which we await His return. Paul wrote that Jesus first came to earth in the fullness of time—it was God's time for Him to come that He might die for our sins.

Peter wrote that God will exalt us in "due time," speaking of the fact that Jesus will again return to earth in God's time. God's plan for us in these days is to be subject one to another in humility in preparation for the return of His Son to be exalted with His saints!

Husband and Wife: A Partnership!

*Wives, in the same way be submissive to
your husands . . . Your beauty should not
come from outward adornment . . .
Instead, it should be that of your inner
self, the unflolding beauty of a gentle and
quiet spirit. . . . Husbands, in the same
way be considerate as you live with your
wives, and treat them with respect.*
(1 Peter 3:1–7)

We have come to a sorry time in history when public speakers—including many preachers—see fit to deal with problems between men and women, husbands and wives, as a kind of humor calling for a bushel of laughs.

Throughout man's existence, the biological positions of the two sexes have remained unchanged, but psychological attitudes and the social relationships have been altered radically.

In recent years there has been a positive and radical revolution with respect to the relationships of the sexes and I think its origin can largely be traced in the United States. It is an impossibility for me to analyze here the impetus and the details of this movement which has been widely acclaimed as seeking "liberation" for women of the world.

The only rule to follow

What I do want to say about the relationships of husbands and wives will boil down to this: for the Christian of either sex, there is only one rule to follow and this is, "What does the Bible say?"

Christians are first of all children of God, and as children of God we are committed to the Word of God. We are committed to a Man and a book, the man being the Lord Jesus Christ and the book, of course, the Holy Scriptures.

When we have discovered what the Bible has to say with finality about any subject and have determined what pleases the Man in the glory, there is no room left for arguments.

In this epistle, Peter makes a plain statement that Christian wives ought to be in subjection to their own husbands, enforcing what the Bible seems to teach in other places—that the man as head of the race is head of the home.

Go back to Genesis and you will find that God made Adam from the dust of the ground and blew the breath of life into his nostrils.

Then, because it was not good for him to be alone, God made the woman from a part of the man—and the woman must understand and accept that.

But, quickly and on the other hand, it must be said that there is absolutely no scriptural authority, neither precept nor biblical example, to allow any husband to behave as a brutal lord, ruling his home with an iron hand.

Read again the story of Abraham and Sarah and you will note the noble leadership of the man Abraham. He never ruled with an iron hand!

Go on to poor Jacob with all of his domestic difficulties. There was always a graciousness and a kindness within his family circle!

You continue through Old Testament history and although it was a bit in the shadows compared with the New Testament, still and nevertheless, there was never any brutal masculine domination in the families with whom God was dealing.

Supplement one another

In your serious study of the Bible as the Word of God, you will have to agree that the Bible seems to teach that the husband and wife should supplement one another. In other words, it seems to be the will of God that husband and wife together may become what neither one could be apart and alone!

Certainly the Bible picture is plain in denying

the husband any right to be a dominating despot delighting in hard-handed dealings with his wife and family.

On the other hand, neither is a dominating and rebellious wife ever recognized nor approved in the Scriptures! An overwhelming and mischievous wife is the product of sin and unbelief and such a role had no place whatsoever in God's will for the Christian family.

There is to be the understanding that two people have entered into a covenant by their choice and by force of circumstance, living in the same home and situation. The understanding should include the fact that the husband, according to the Scripture and the will of God, is the head of the race and the home, but that he should function wisely, according to Peter's gentle admonition: "Husbands, in the same way be considerate as you live with your wives."

Peter is advising the husband to use his head and the common sense he has been given: " . . . treat them with respect as the weaker partner and as heirs with you of the gracious gift of life" (1 Peter 3:7b).

In other words, husband and wife are children of God together, equal heirs of the grace of life.

If we will remember this fact prayerfully, I think we will become aware that it is at this point that chivalry was born! I am speaking of Christian chivalry, as we understand it.

The world in which we live and the society of which we are a part have often sought to lampoon and satirize the concept of woman as the weaker vessel. There have been thousands of jokes, and cartoonists have had a field day with their drawings of the buxom woman leading the meek, little lamb-of-a-man down the street.

But we remember that the Scriptures say that the man and the woman are heirs together of the grace of life. Husband and wife, if both are Christians, are Christian heirs together! They are united in their strongest bond—they are one in Jesus Christ, their Savior!

Now, Peter makes a very strong comment in this passage for the benefit of husbands. He says that if husbands do not treat their wives with consideration and respect their prayers will be hindered.

I suppose there are many Christian husbands whose prayers are not being answered and they can think up lots of reasons. But the fact is that thoughtless husbands are simply big, overbearing clods when it comes to consideration of their wives.

Live according to knowledge

If the husband would get himself straightened out in his own mind and spirit and live with his wife according to knowledge, and treat her with the chivalry that belongs to her as the weaker vessel, remembering that she is actually his sister in Christ, his prayers would be answered in spite of the devil and all of the other reasons that he gives.

A husband's spiritual problems do not lie in the Kremlin nor in the Vatican but in the heart of the man himself—in attitude and inability to resist the temptation to grumble and growl and dominate!

There is no place for that kind of male rulership in any Christian home. What the Bible calls for is proper and kindly recognition of the true relationships of understanding and love, and the acceptance of a spirit of cooperation between the husband and wife.

An unbelieving spouse

Peter also seeks to give us a plain answer in this passage concerning the life and conduct of a Christian wife who has an unbelieving and scornful husband.

We dare not deal with this only as a problem out of ancient history. In all of our congregations, we do face the question of the Christian wife: "How do I adjust my Christian life so that I can be obedient to the Scriptures while I am living with a man who hates God and showers me with grumbling and abuse when I insist that I am going to God's house?"

First, we must admit that there is the kind of woman who talks about praying for her husband, but she will never live to see him converted because she refuses the scriptural position that God has given her, and more bluntly because her husband has never seen any spiritual characteristics in her life that he would want for himself!

Peter could hardly give Christian wives any plainer counsel: "Wives, in the same way be submissive to your husbands so that, if any of them do not believe the word, they may be won over without words by the behavior of their wives, when they see the purity and reverence of your lives" (1 Peter 3:1–2).

The scriptural advice is to this effect: that the quiet, cooperative Christian wife is a powerful instrument for good in the home, and without too many words, is still an evangelist hard to resist. Peter strongly infers that the man, seemingly rejecting her doctrine and laughing at her faith, is badly smitten deep in his own conscience by her meek and quiet spirit and her chaste conversation coupled with godly fear.

In summary, we have mentioned two extremes—the harsh husband whose prayers are not answered, and the wife whose life does not show consistent godliness and patience in adversity.

I thank God that in between those two positions there are great throngs of good, decent people trying to do the best they can for God in their life situations, overlooking the obvious irritations and together experiencing the grace of God!

I thank God indeed for that great number of believing men and women who get along together in Christ's bonds and with the help of the Spirit of God succeed in establishing a consistent example to their families, their neighbors and their friends!

I am aware that at about this point some of you are wondering if I will ignore the rest of Peter's admonition to the Christian women of his day.

There is a problem in this passage, but I may die tomorrow and I would not want to die knowing that only a day before I had been too cowardly and timid to deal with a text of Scripture!

Counsel to wives

Here it is, in Peter's counsel to the wives:

> Your beauty should not come from outward adornment, such as braided hair and the wearing of gold jewelry and fine clothes. Instead, it should be that of your inner self. (3:3–4a)

First, notice the manner in which Peter lifts the entire questions up and beyond the plane where there is division between the sexes and puts the matter on a spiritual plane where there is no division and where it is the hidden being of the heart and the spirit that really matters.

Second, what does the Bible really teach here about the outward adorning of the person?

It says that the woman is not to seek to be attractive by outward adorning and dress. Does it expressly forbid the braiding of the hair, the wearing of gold and the putting on of fine clothes? This is a question often asked.

Let's say "yes" and then go on from there and see where we stand.

When I was a boy every little girl had a pigtail that came to her hips. The longer the pigtail the prouder the girl!

Does the Bible say, then, that a woman must not be adorned with braided hair?

If we say, "Yes, that's what it means"—that rules out the braiding of your hair.

The advice continues: "Let it not be the wearing of gold."

Does that mean that gold can never be worn in any way by a Christian woman?

We will agree for the moment and say that gold is out!

"Nor the putting on of fine clothes."

Now, wait a minute! We are in trouble with our reasoning here, because this certainly does not mean that the woman is not to put on any nice clothes.

If it doesn't mean a strict ban on fixing the hair or wearing of gold or putting on of fine clothes, what does it mean?

It means the true attractiveness of the person is not outward but inward! Therefore, the Christian woman should remember that she cannot buy true attractiveness—that radiance which really shines forth in beauty is of the heart and spirit and not of the body!

That is what Peter meant and anything else by way of exclusion or structure is of narrow, private interpretation and will lead into an unloving fanaticism!

There is not one line of expression here that would lead us to believe that Peter was laying down the law that it is wrong for a woman to braid her hair. The women know they have to do something with it!

Nor is there anything in the Scripture that teaches that the use of gold is forbidden in proper ways. God in creation made gold and strung it all around. It is pretty to look at and it is an element in itself. If we have any of it and can afford it, there is nothing in the Scripture that says "Don't wear it" any more than it says, "Don't wear fine clothes!"

Don't let apparel be your attractiveness

So, the teaching is plain: don't let your apparel be your true attractiveness. Don't try to substitute gold jewelry for the true beauty of the being!

I am sure that we would not be mistaken to presume that Peter had a reason for writing this, for history bears out the fact that there were customs and fads and styles in those days, too.

I suppose it was the vogue and the thing to do—make the braided hair a kind of work of art, with great displays of gold and jewelry and fine apparel among the worldly and unsaved women of that pagan time.

Perhaps Peter sounds a trifle sour to some when he writes and says, "You Christian women are a different kind of person than you were before you knew the Lord. As Christians you should be more interested in character and inward spiritual life than in your clothing and adornment."

Slovenly habits and appearance

Having said this about the true inward attractiveness of the person, it must also be said that no Christian woman should ever sink into slovenly habits of dress and appearance. How can it be possible for any Christian woman, carrying her big Bible and teacher's quarterly, to become known as a proverbial "dowd"?

She cannot impress me with her professed spirituality. I can only shrug and think about her unkempt dress: "Did she go to the old bureau in the attic and pull out the old rag or did she sleep in it?"

I can be very positive about this—I don't believe that true spirituality can afford to leave that kind of slovenly impression. There is no place in the heart of Jesus Christ nor in that of the tender, artistic Holy Ghost for dowdiness nor dirt nor inconsistency!

I remember the account of the old Quaker brother who had to make a call at the home of one of the Christian sisters in his city. They greeted one another in the traditional dignified manner of the Quakers and then had a brief conversation about the things of God.

As he was about to leave, she said, "Brother, would you care to pray with me before you go?"

He said, "No," and she said, "Why?"

He answered, "Your house is dirty and God never told me to get down on my knees in a dirty house. Clean up your house and I will come back and pray."

Perhaps she had been too busy praying to keep the house clean, but I believe an orderly and well-kept house would have helped her Christian testimony, and perhaps she could have prayed better, as well.

Four simple words

Now, there has to be some sort of outward adorning and I would summarize it in four familiar words: *clean, neat, modest, appropriate.*

None can say that they do not understand the word *clean.* However poor we may be, we may still be clean. Nearly everyone has enough water available for basic cleanliness.

Why can't we all be neat in our daily contacts? I do not think anyone ever needs to look as though he had gone through a cyclone and had no time since to get "accumulated."

In our day, some folks seen to think the word *modest* is a comical word. You can laugh it off if you want to, but it is one of the words that we will face in that great day of coming judgment.

In our Christian lives, we should know the strength of the word *appropriate*. I think every Christian woman should dress appropriately, properly and suitably to her circumstances and to her income. A Christian woman who tries to give out tracts dressed in loud, flashy apparel or in dirty and disheveled garb will be a poor advertisement for the gospel she is trying to proclaim publicly!

I realize that some women excuse their manner of dress in public by the fact that they have so little money to spend for clothing.

I contend that a woman still doesn't have to be grotesque in her garb even though she must wrestle with the problems of small income.

You know that I ride the public buses occasionally and for the small price of the fare it is a wonderful place to observe human nature.

When I see some of the inappropriate and grotesque things worn by women boarding the buses I have wondered why others in the family did not protest: "Please, Mama, don't go out like that! People will think you have escaped."

I think there is a great contradiction apparent among us. Many women are working so hard in all kinds of jobs that they are making themselves old in the effort to get money enough to buy the clothes and cosmetics that are supposed to make them look young.

As far as I am concerned, it does not reflect

any credit on the common sense or spirituality of any woman who knowingly goes beyond her financial bracket to decorate herself for the sake of appearance!

A proper model of character

Finally, I think that a Christian woman must be careful about the kind of person she sets up as a model of character and example in daily life. It is a sad thing to have our minds occupied with the wrong kind of people.

I don't think English history books will ever report that Suzanna Wesley was one of the best-dressed women of her day or that she ever received a medal for social activity. But she was the mother of Charles and John Wesley, those princes of Christian song and theology. She taught her own family, and her spiritual life and example have placed her name high in God's hall of fame for all eternity.

So, if you want to take models to follow day by day, please do not take the artificial, globe-trotting females who are intent only upon themselves, their careers and their publicity. Rather, take Sarah, the princess who gave her love and obedience to Abraham; or Suzanna Wesley or Florence Nightingale, Clara Barton or Mary Fuller.

There are so many good examples and it is a serious matter, for the judgment shall declare every person's faith and work and influence!

I have not been trying just to fill the role of a

feminine counselor, but to remind you that the Apostle Peter, a great man of God, said it all a long time ago! True adorning is the lasting beauty that is within. It is the glowing but hidden being of the heart, more radiant than all of the jewels that one can buy!

God help us all, men and women of whatever marital, social or domestic status, that we may do the will of God and thus win our crown!

Trust God with Your Emotions!

Wherefore gird up the loins of your mind,
be sober, and hope to the end for the grace
that is to be brought unto you at the
revelation of Jesus Christ.
(1 Peter 1:13, KJV)

We are in the good company of the apostles when we seek to put in a word for reason in the expression of our Christian life and character.

Peter and the other New Testament preachers were fervent in their exhortations to Christian believers that they should always exhibit the loftiest kind of spirituality regardless of the human circumstances.

Why did Peter, then, add a practical dimension of caution that the child of God should "gird up the loins of [his] mind" and be sober-minded in the daily expression of his Christian worship and witness?

It is my interpretation that the apostle was cautioning the believers that their human emotions were not to be allowed to get out of control. I think he was pleading for the kind of spirituality that comes with the filling of the Holy Spirit and is marked by our walking in heavenly places in Christ Jesus, and certainly is not degraded by dethronement of the sentinel we call reason!

The spirit of the prophet is always subject to the prophet. When the Spirit of God moves into a man's heart, He will never make a fool out of him. He will make the man happy but He will never make him silly. He may make him sad with the woe and the weight of the world's grief but He will never let him become a gloomy cynic. The Holy Spirit will make him warm-hearted and responsive but He will never cause him to do things of which he will be ashamed later.

Peter was not promoting or predicting a cold and lifeless and formal spirituality in the Christian church when he advised believers to gird up the loins of their minds and be sober.

He was saying to the early Christians as he hopes to say to us now: "Brethren, if ever there was an hour when we needed to be serious about our Christian faith, this is the hour! We need to be sober men—and spiritual men!"

No Christian church ought to be a mere tombstone, even though the tombstone is probably the most sober of all things. A tombstone will just continue to sit throughout the years, showing no change whether in cold or wind or snow or heat, in peacetime or in war, no matter what the developments in history.

The tombstone just sits there, always in the same orthodox position, faithfully reminding the passing visitor that Mr. John M. Jones 1861–1932, lies there. That's the story and witness of the tombstone!

I admit that there are some churches like that. In order to keep sober and formal and quiet, they are contented to stay dead! But that is not the kind of church that Peter would have chosen and neither is it the kind of congregation with which we want to be identified.

Peter had some basis of concern for writing to Christian believers with this expression of caution and the Holy Spirit has seen fit to pass it along to us. I think we see in this the Bible method.

The Bible, like everything else God has made, has method in it. I can see His method in the fact that this Bible verse begins with the connecting word, "Wherefore." It looks back at something that is to be done.

The biblical method is to lay down strong foundations of truth and these foundations of truth are declarations of God. Principally, they are declarations of what God is doing or has done, or both.

Then, after this foundation has been laid, it is

the Holy Spirit's method and desire to show that this revealed truth constitutes a moral obligation.

It is at this point that I am in controversy with some elements of leadership in our Christian churches today. It is my considered opinion that one of the greatest weaknesses in the modern church is the willingness to lay down foundations   of truth without ever backing them up with moral application!

Must have moral application

The great American evangelist, Charles Finney, went so far as to declare bluntly that it is sinful to teach the Bible without moral application. He asked what good is accomplished merely to study a course in the Bible to find out what it says, if there is to be no obligation to do anything as a result of what has been learned?

There can be a right and a wrong emphasis in conducting Bible classes. I am convinced that some Bible classes are nothing more than a means whereby men become even more settled in their religious prejudices.

Only when we have moral application are we in the Bible method!

When we give ourselves seriously to Bible study, we discover the Holy Spirit's method.

"This is what God did, and this is what God did. Therefore, this is what you ought to do!" That is always the Bible way.

You will not find a single book of the Bible

that does not have godly exhortation. There is not a single Bible portion that God wants us to study just to get a cranium full of knowledge or learning.

Moral application of spiritual truth

The Bible always presents the truth and then makes the application: "Now, if this is true, you ought to do something about it!" That is the meaning of moral application of spiritual truth.

In the case before us, Peter had just recited some of the great and gracious things God has done:

> Praise be to the God and Father of our Lord Jesus Christ! In his great mercy he has given us new birth into a living hope through the resurrection of Jesus Christ from the dead, and into an inheritance that can never perish, spoil or fade. (1 Peter 1:3–4)

"Therefore," he continues, "prepare your minds [gird up your loins, KJV] for action; be self-controlled; set your hope fully on the grace to be given you when Jesus Christ is revealed" (1:13).

Girding up the loins is a biblical figure of speech. Peter did not have to explain it because everyone knew what he meant by the analogy. It had to do with their manner of dress.

People wore a kind of tunic in those days, a Mother Hubbard style of garb, we might say. Some of these garments were simply like a blanket with a hole cut in the middle and then strung down over the body.

In a sense, this flowing garb was always in the way, whether the person was working or walking. The tunic was always in the way so it was handled in this manner: if the person was very poor, he simply took a piece of dry leather and cut it in such a way that it could be tied around the waist and pulled into a loop. In this fashion, the person was girded.

With that belt or girdle tied and holding the garment close to the body, a person could run or walk or travel or climb or work and the garment did not hinder either hands or feet.

There is a good New Testament illustration that we all remember. John the Baptist came to his ministry wearing a cumbersome tunic made of camel's hair. He was a man of great activity, but he was a poor man. We are told that he girded his garment with a leather girdle. The rich and the affluent were able to use more expensive woven belts and girdles, but they accomplished the same thing—freedom of feet and hands for necessary walking and activity in everyday life.

Peter tells the Christian believers that they are to gird up the loins of their minds.

I trust no one holds the idea that our minds are not a part of our inner life.

Let us deal with this principle first insofar as it relates to the natural man, unconverted persons, the sons and daughters of Adam and Eve.

In general, the natural man born into this world and growing up in it, regardless of his rank or station, education or possessions, will be by his very nature indifferent and careless and disorganized within his inner life.

Popular and accepted manner of life

The popular and accepted manner of life is followed by the average man, not because he thinks that is all there is, but because he really doesn't think about it at all.

Even a sinner, if he really gives himself to serious thoughts, will rebel against the tyranny of the popular and accepted ways. There have been many unconverted men throughout history who rebelled against the ways and the manner of the day in which they lived. I admire independence of spirit in men, for it takes a serious-thinking man to stand up and refuse to bow and bend; but the average man will not give himself to this kind of stern thinking.

The average man has only petty things to think about: Is there enough time left on that matter?

Who will win the World Series? How much profit will I make on this deal?

He does not give himself to thought about those things that touch character, that seek to touch his inner life. He keeps everything on the shallow surface of his life—that's the sinner I am talking about.

The sinner is careless and disorganized and indifferent, except for the area where he has to tighten up his belt. He may be an expert in some field—mathematics, science, industry or business—and in his field he is forced to do some careful thinking, but it does not reach over into moral thinking. It is not the kind of thinking that will touch his inner life or his conduct.

The average man's life is all ungirded and ragged and at loose ends while he is carefully thinking and applying himself in his own prescribed field. He has never learned to think through to the truth and then make the necessary personal application to his own needs, his own standard, his own person.

Peter insists that it is the converted, born-again men and women who are to gird up the loins of their minds.

I do not believe we do Peter any injustice to infer that he expected this to be one of the first things we will do after we are converted to Jesus Christ—to gird up our minds and become sensitive to eternal values!

Two aspects

There were two aspects of girding up the loins in the Old Testament figure of speech. First was the preparation for working and toiling without hinderance, and second was readi-

ness for sudden departure and travel. Both
Peter and Paul use this phrase in urging
spiritual preparation and readiness in writing
to New Testament Christians.

It is only after we yield to Jesus Christ and
begin to follow Him that we become concerned
about the laxity and thoughtlessness of our
daily lives. We begin to grieve about the way
we have been living and we become convicted
that there should continue to be aimlessness
and futility and carelessness in our Christian
walk.

I have been forced to admit that one of the
things hardest for me to understand and try to
reconcile is the complete aimlessness of so
many Christians' lives.

They certainly are not shooting directly at
anything, so if they should hit it, they would
not know it, anyhow! Many of their lives are at
loose ends. They are not girded up!

Probably the worst part of this situation
among us is the fact that so many of our Christian brothers and sisters have unusual gifts and
talents and capacities—yet they have not exer-
cised this discipline of girding up the mind and
spiritual potential in order to make the necessary progress in the Christian life.

Why should a pastor have to confess total
failure from year to year? Why should he have
to go from one church to another, starting
something, trying something—only to admit
failure again?

I don't think he has ever really girded himself. He has abilities but they are not disciplined. He has a fine mind but it is not girded up. He is like a man with a treasured Stradivarius violin that has never been put in tune. He has never taken time to sit down and tune that priceless instrument, therefore he gets no melody and harmony from it.

Must be sober and thoughtful

All Christians must be sober and thoughtful at this point of carelessness and looseness. Twenty years from now, what assessment will be made of our Christian lives, our maturity and spiritual growth and progress? Will someone say of us: "He's the same old man—a little thicker, a little balder, a little heavier—but he has made no progress in his inner spiritual life. He failed to grow and mature because he never learned the discipline of girding up."

I fully believe that it was Peter's expectation that laxity and carelessness and aimlessness would all be repudiated and forsaken by the serious-minded Christian believer.

What does this say to the average Christian who refuses to think about these factors because they will touch his moral and spiritual life?

I am thinking here of the average Christian as I have known him. He is willing to make a gesture of brief meditation, but only enough to ease his conscience, and then he reverts back to his aimless life. In spiritual matters, he is actually tossed around like a cork on the waves, a puppet of circumstances. He does not know what it means to navigate a straight course for God, like a ship on her way to the harbor.

We have been schooled theologically to excuse this kind of Christian life on the basis of weakness and frailty, and we tell ourselves that it is not really sinful. Personally, I think there must be some kind of limit to the time that believers can continue their selfish and aimless habits of life without bordering on sin!

Actually, I think that we can get so prodigal with our talents and so careless with our time and so aimless with our activities that we will be faced with the fact of sin in our lives—for we know what we should do and what we should be, but we would rather excuse our failure!

The book of Proverbs tells us about the man who lies on his bed, turning like a door on its hinges, while the weeds grow up in his garden, choking and killing his crop. Then, when harvest has come, he has nothing and is reduced to begging for help.

Now, staying in bed when he should be cultivating his garden may not be overly sinful—but I think there is no argument but what a willfully lazy man is a sinful man.

It follows then, in my estimation, that a person who is intellectually lazy is a sinful person. God had a reason for giving us our heads with intellectual capacity for thinking and reasoning and considering. But what a great company of humans there are who refuse to use their heads and many of these are Christians, we must confess.

Many a preacher would like to challenge the intellectual and thinking capacity of his congregation, but he has been warned about preaching over the people's heads.

I ask, "What are people's heads for? God Almighty gave them those heads and I think they ought to use them!"

Truth never goes over heads

As a preacher, I deny that any of the truths of God which I teach and expound are over the heads of the people. I deny it!

My preaching may go right through their heads if there is nothing in there to stop it, but I do not preach truths which are too much for them to comprehend. We ought to begin using our heads. Brother, you ought to take that head of yours, oil it and rub the rust off and begin to use it as God has always expected you would. God expects you to understand and have a grasp of His truth because you need it from day to day.

I have been reading in the works of the saintly Nicholas Herman, better known to us as Brother Lawrence. He recommends that Christian believers should nourish their hearts on high and noble thoughts of God. The question revolves around our daily use of our minds and thought life—sensational magazines and soap operas and doubtful stories will forever keep us from nourishing our hearts on noble thoughts of God!

The Holy Spirit knows us well and enforces the exhortation to gird up our minds, to pull up our spiritual standards, to eliminate carelessness in word and thought and deed, and in activities and interest!

Now, let us think of what Peter must have had in mind when he added the words, "be sober," to the discipline of right thinking.

Sobriety is that human attitude of mind when calm reason is in control. The mind is balanced and cool and the feelings are subject to reason and this statement is proof enough for me that the Holy Spirit will never urge believers into any kind of spiritual experience that violates and dethrones reason.

All of us are aware of instances where men and women have taken part in unreasonable and unseemly acts and then excused them on the grounds that they were moved by the Spirit.

Frankly, I must doubt that! I doubt that the Holy Ghost ever moves to dethrone reason in any man's mind.

In regard to my own personal and spiritual life, I must testify that the highest, loftiest and most God-beholding moments in my own experience have been so calm that I could write

about them, so peaceful that I could tell about
them and analyze them.

Always in control

I do believe that the human reason, blessed
and warmed and shining with the love of God,
must always be in control.

Think of the completely opposite picture, that
of drunkenness. If you walk past the corner
bar, you are likely to find a fellow staggering
out of the bar, drunken to the point that reason
has actually been dethroned and human judgment is completely impaired.

Someone a long time ago called liquor "a liq-
uid damnation" and wrote about the man who
opens his mouth and drinks down something
that makes "his brains go out." Actually, the
emotions get completely out of control—that's
what happens to a drunk man.

Out of control—and the first sign is that he
gets too happy and talkative. Then he gets af-
fectionate and generally with people whom he
did not even know until an hour earlier.

Then he will probably get sad, and because
his emotions are out of control, he wants to tell
the bartender and everyone who will listen
about the wife who doesn't understand him
and the family that doesn't appreciate him.

That's what liquor does for many unthinking,
weak and careless people in our day; it robs
them of all control of their emotions and judgment. Most of them are sorry and embarrassed

and ashamed the morning after; but they refuse to thoughtfully gird up their minds, so weakness becomes a pattern.

The Apostle Paul stands with Peter in this serious-minded approach to the use of our faculties under the guidance and blessing of the Holy Spirit. He wrote to the Ephesian church with a caution to be wise in the understanding of the will of the Lord and advises them:

> Do not get drunk on wine, which leads to debauchery. Instead be filled with the Spirit. Speak to one another with psalms, hymns and spiritual songs. Sing and make music in your heart to the Lord, always giving thanks to God the Father for everything, in the name of our Lord Jesus Christ. (Ephesians 5:18–20)

Peter and Paul thus join in urging us to practice and display the loftiest fruits of the Spirit of God with the Spirit Himself in control of our emotions and our affections, our worship and our praise. Yes, brothers, the Spirit will make the believing child of God generous but He will never make him foolish! He will make him happy but He will never make him silly! The Spirit will warm the inner life of the Christian's being but he will never lead him to do the things that would cause him to hang his head in shame afterward.

Thank God for enduring joy

I say "Thank God" for the kind of enduring joy which comes to the believer whose emotional life is in the keeping of the Spirit. I stand with the dear child of God whose reason is sanctified and who refuses to be swept from his mooring in the Word of God either by the latest popular vogue in religious fad or the ascendence of the most recent sensational personality in gospel circles.

The child of God will not be swept away by fear nor feeling nor love of anything earthly; he is sailing by the stars!

The illustration is about the young sailor who was pressed into service at the helm of the ship.

"You see that bright star?" he was asked. "Just keep that star a little off your port bow and you will stay right on course."

But when the ship's officer returned, the sailor had the ship far off course.

"Why didn't you keep your course by that star?" he was asked.

"Oh, I passed that star miles back," he responded.

Well, he had lost his star, and some of God's people in our churches are showing a lot of impatience with our determination, by the grace of God, to navigate with His star out there ahead of us.

I confess that we do not have as much

popularity and acclaim and we do not preach to the largest crowds and there never seems to be excess money floating around, but we are looking with hope to the future. In the long run, it will be something very precious to know that when men's minds were all at loose ends and going to pieces, we were able to gird up the loins of our minds by the help of our Lord Jesus Christ!

We are not Christian dreamers engaging in idle and wishful thinking. We know who we are and to whom we belong and we know where we are going. Ours is a forward look in hope and expectation and we are surely among those whom Paul describes in writing to the Thessalonian church:

> So then, let us not be like others, who are asleep, but let us be alert and self-control-led. For those who sleep, sleep at night, and those who get drunk, get drunk at night. But since we belong to the day, let us be self-controlled, putting on faith and love as a breastplate, and the hope of salvation as a helmet. For God did not appoint us to suffer wrath but to receive salvation through our Lord Jesus Christ. (1 Thessalonians 5:6–9)

Amen! We are looking forward to it because God Himself has said it by His Spirit, and He cannot lie!

The Christian Has a Right to Grin!

*In this you greatly rejoice, though now
for a little while you may have had to
suffer grief in all kinds of trials.*
(1 Peter 1:6)

I have always felt compassion for Christian men and women who seem to major in pessimism, looking on the dark and gloomy side and never able to do anything with life's problems but grumble about them!

I meet them often, and when I do I wonder: "Can these people be reading the same Bible that I have been reading?"

Peter wrote to the tempted, suffering and persecuted believers in his day and noted with thanksgiving that they could rejoice because they counted God's promises and provision greater then their trials. They looked for a future state of things which would be much better than any current situation on this earth.

Now, I know that in any church setting it is possible to find Christians who are intent upon a wrong emphasis in either of two directions.

First, there are always those who are taken up entirely with the emphasis of the sweet bye and bye. They are contented with getting by on a spiritual appeal of "Come now—and wait for the feast!"

In spiritual matters, they are much like the little boy whose mother says, "Johnnie, here is a piece of bread and butter. We will not be eating for another hour, you know."

Johnnie probably has a ravenous appetite, but in this instance he is forced to piece out his hunger until the dinner is finally ready.

Some Christians seem satisfied to go along without even a slice—but on a bare crumb! They are putting all of their emphasis on the feast to come in the sweet bye and bye.

But, on the other hand, there are those who make the mistake of putting all of the emphasis upon the "sweet now and now," therefore thinking very little about the world to come.

I am sure this brings the question: "What, then, is the proper emphasis?"

The right thing to do is to put the emphasis where God put it—and I think that is the emphasis that there are some things you can have now and some things you cannot have now!

I insist that the Lord expects His people to be thorough and sincere students of the Bible so that we will not be guilty of surrendering anything that is promised for us now or demanding anything presently that is promised as a later benefit. There would be a lot less tension among believers and much less nervous pressure and misunderstanding if we would study our Bible with that thought in mind!

Actually, there is no promise of any such thing as absolute perfection now. Perfection is a relative thing now and God has not really completed a thing with us, as yet.

Absolute perfection is for the time when the sons of God shall be revealed and completeness awaits the time when we shall look upon the Son and become grown-up sons, indeed. Peter said that the persecuted and suffering Christians of his day looked for a state of things immeasurably better than that which they knew, and that state of things would be perfect and complete!

What great changes

Oh, what great changes there will be when we come to that time of perfect completeness and complete perfection!

The very earth itself and all of nature surrounding us will reveal the blessings of God's perfection in that coming time.

The Apostle Paul, speaking as the man of God, tries to tell us how the realm of nature will be changed, in the Epistle to the Romans:

I consider that our present sufferings are

not worth comparing with the glory that will be revealed in us. The creation waits in eager expectation for the sons of God to be revealed. For the creation was subjected to frustration, not by its own choice, but by the will of the one who subjected it, in hope that the creation itself will be liberated from its bondage to decay and brought into the glorious freedom of the children of God. We know that the whole creation has been groaning as in the pains of childbirth right up to the present time. Not only so, but we ourselves, who have the firstfruits of the Spirit, groan inwardly as we wait eagerly for our adoption as sons, the redemption of our bodies. (8:18–23).

Paul is trying to make it plain to us that mankind is so related to the earth that when the Lord comes in triumph to glorify mankind, He will also glorify the earth and nature. He insists that the earth and nature will share in the glorification with the sons of God who were once sons of Adam but are now children of the King.

This old earth, as we know it, did go down in a collapse with the sons of Adam when we all went down together. Floods and typhoons and earthquakes, tornadoes and tidal waves are all the result of the distorted state of fallen nature. Sickness and insanity and all of our weaknesses and frailties in the flesh can be traced to this fallen state of affairs for we are still very much a part of the earth and of nature.

Man and his home—this earth—are very much alike and so God will redeem the earth by redeeming people. In the hour that He comes to glorify redeemed mankind, He will also allow that glorification to overflow and spread throughout the earth!

That means, also, that great changes in human society will be wrought in that day of completeness and perfection.

We could read for hours in the Old Testament, noting the quotations which look forward to that day in which the earth will be full of the knowledge of the Lord, illustrated by the manner in which we know the waters cover the sea.

A different kind of society

There will be a kind of human society which we have not yet known. There will no longer be great problems between management and labor and between landlords and tenants because "No man will build and another inhabit."

There will be no need for rent ceilings and price controls. There will be no need for people to live in rat-infested tenements because everything will belong to God and everyone will possess his own land and live in his own house.

There will be no problem concerning labor and toil because one will not plant and another reap but every man will reap what he plants! God will take care of that for the earth will be full of the knowledge of the Lord.

The believing children of God should have an optimistic outlook about God's future plans for this earth and human society, based upon the realities expressed in the prophetic Scriptures. We cannot accept man's own horrible predictions of destruction, which range from this earth falling into the sun to destruction by a runaway comet sweeping the earth to a dreadful fate.

As Christians and students of the Word of God, we believe that this earth is yet to be the home of a redeemed people and a changed society that will recognize His lordship.

Also, for Christian believers, it is a more personal note to learn from the Bible that the great day of perfection and rejoicing will bring great changes, affecting our bodies, our minds and souls.

The Apostle John clearly spoke to Christian believers when he wrote:

> Dear friends, now we are the children of God, and what we will be has not yet been made known. But we know that when he appears, we shall be like him, for we shall see him as he is. (1 John 3:2)

Then the Apostle Paul, in spite of the imperfection of language, gave the Corinthian Christians the divinely inspired description of great changes to be wrought in bodies of the believing children of God in that great day of revelation and transformation:

> But someone may ask, "How are the dead raised? With what kind of body will they come?" (1 Corinthians 15:35)

At this point, Paul was not quite as patient with questions as he might have been. He answered:

> How foolish! What you sow does not come to life unless it dies. When you sow, you do not plant the body that will be, but just a seed, perhaps of wheat or of something else. But God gives it a body as he has determined, and to each kind of seed he gives its own body. All flesh is not the same: Men have one kind of flesh, animals have another, birds another and fish another. There are also heavenly bodies and there are earthly bodies; but the splendor of the heavenly bodies is one kind, and the splendor of the earthly bodies is another. The sun has one kind of splendor, the moon another and the stars another; and star differs from star in splendor.
> So will it be with the resurrection of the

dead. The body that is sown is perishable, it is raised imperishable; it is sown in dishonor, it is raised in glory; it is sown in weakness, it is raised in power; it is sown a natural body, it is raised a spiritual body.

If there is a natural body, there is also a spiritual body. So it is written: "The first man Adam became a living being"; the last Adam, a life-giving spirit. The spiritual did not come first, but the natural, and after that the spiritual. The first man was of the dust of the earth, the second man from heaven. As was the earthly man, so are those who are of the earth; and as is the man from heaven, so are those who are of heaven. And just as we have borne the likeness of the earthly man, so shall we bear the likeness of the man from heaven. (36–49)

These are among the reasons that believing Christians, whether in the apostolic time or in our own, may be expected to have an optimistic and cheerful outlook, waiting for salvation which shall be revealed in the last time and engaged in great rejoicing as they wait!

This note of rejoicing is very clear throughout the entire Bible and in the New Testament it rings forth like a silver bell.

Never a life of gloom

The life of the normal, believing child of God

can never become a life of gloom and pessimism. In every age we will have some people whose concept of Christianity is a kind of gloomy resignation to the inevitable. But it is the Holy Spirit who has promised the ability for the Christian to rejoice in God's promises day by day.

Of course, the Christian believer is serious minded and he can weep with those who weep. But he is alert and optimistic and has a cheerful hope because he is looking for that changed state of affairs which is so far beyond anything that this world has to offer.

Peter states it as a paradox: the obedient Christian greatly rejoices even in the midst of great heaviness, trials and suffering. God's people know that things here are not all they ought to be, but they are not spending any time in worrying about it. They are too busy rejoicing in the gracious prospect of all that will take place when God fulfills all of His promises to His redeemed children!

This leads us directly into a summary of the glorious contradictions which make the life of the Christian such a puzzle to the worldling. We must admit that the true Christian is a rather strange person in the eye of the unbeliever.

I use the adjective *true* in regard to the Christian not only to point out the necessity for the new birth but to indicate, also, the Christian who is living according to his new birth. I speak here of a transformed life pleasing to God, for if you want to be a Christian, you must agree to a very much different life. The life of obedience to Jesus Christ means living moment by moment in the Spirit of God and it will be so different from your former life that you will often be considered strange. In fact, the life in the Spirit is such a different life that some of your former associates will probably discuss the question of whether or not you are mentally disturbed. The true Christian may seem a strange person indeed to those who make their observations only from the point of view of this present world, which is alienated from God and His gracious plan of salvation.

Consider now these glorious contradictions and you will no longer wonder why the true believer in Jesus Christ is such an amazement to this world.

The Christian is dead and yet he lives forever. He died to himself and yet he lives in Christ.

The reason he lives is because of the death of another.

Save your life by losing it

The Christian saves his own life by losing it and he is in danger of losing it by trying to save it.

It is an interesting thing that when he wants to get up, the Christian always starts down, for God's way up is always down, even though that is contrary to common sense. It is also contrary to the finest wisdom on the earth, because the foolish things of God are wiser than anything on this earth.

He always surrenders

You may also note about the true Christian that when he wants to sin, he always surrenders. Instead of standing and slugging it out, he surrenders to a third party and wins without firing a shot or receiving a bruise. He surrenders to God and so wins over everyone else!

Another strange thing about him is that he is strongest when he is weakest and weakest when he is strongest. It is God's principle in his life that his strength lies in his weakness for when he gets up thinking that he is strong he is always weak. However, when he gets down on his knees thinking he is weak, he is always strong!

Again, he may be poor—and if he is a real Christian, he usually is—and yet he will always make others rich. Paul was a poor man in prison, but he immeasurably enriched the entire Christian world. John Bunyan was a poor man in Bedford jail, but he gave us *Pilgrim's Progress.*

You can go on down the scale throughout history and you will find that a rich Christian was generally poor and the poor Christian made everyone rich.

This man who is a true Christian is at his

highest when he feels the lowest and he is lowest when he feels the highest. He is in the least danger when he is fearful and trusting God, and in most danger when he feels the most self-confident.

He is most sinless when he feels the most sinful and he is the most sinful when he feels the most sinless.

Yes, he is a strange fellow, this Christian! He has the most when he is giving away the most and he has less when he is keeping most. That is contrary to the common sense of this world and that is why we are considered a peculiar group of people—but they don't know us!

When they try to figure it out, they cannot get the true picture.

A man will say, "Well, I am willing to believe and to go to church at Christmas and on Mother's Day, but I cannot understand this strange fanatic who seems to have the most when he is giving the most!"

He has never discerned God's principle of blessing the nine-tenths which the Christian has for himself so that it is actually more than the ten-tenths without any provision for God or His causes.

Here's a strange thing about the Christian believer. He sometimes is doing the most when he is not doing anything at all. Sometimes to get the most done, God calls him to the side and says, "Sit down there." Sometimes he goes the fastest when he is standing still for in faith he may hear the whisper: "Stand still and see the salvation of the Lord!"

Saved now and later

One of the important principles in the Christian's daily life is this: he is saved now and is ready to declare it with shining face and yet he expects to be saved later! He is continually looking for a salvation ready to be revealed in the last time.

We must look at this for someone is sure to say, "Make up your mind! Is he saved now or is he anticipating salvation?"

Of course he is saved now; but he is also looking to be saved. He has life now, but he is also looking for the perfection to be revealed in the future plan of God. Now, you will not be able to explain that to your neighbor; he will just underscore the fact that it is part of your strange religious fanaticism. He does not understand that you are a true Christian!

Neither will the world ever understand our insistence that the Christian born on this earth is actually a citizen of another country which he has not yet visited. He is born on earth and yet he knows by faith that he is a citizen of heaven.

The Bible tells us plainly that while we are walking on this earth we are seated in the heavenly places in Christ Jesus our Lord—and that doesn't refer to the midweek prayer service! It means that by faith and spiritual position in Christ we are seated in the heavenly places.

The believer knows that in himself he is nothing, but even while he is humbly telling the Lord that he is nothing, he knows very well that he is the apple of God's eye!

Some of our critics say: "You Christians talk about yourself and your relation to God as if you were God's very best."

I have a good answer to that, too! The very Christian who believes that he is the apple of God's eye is the same unselfish Christian who is giving sacrificially of his money, sending his sons and daughters or going himself to preach the gospel to the least and the last of the peoples of the earth!

Finally, the good Christian is in love with one he has never seen, and although he fears and reveres God, he is not afraid of God at all!

Many of the philosophers and poets phrased it all wrong when they tried to advise everyone on earth not to be afraid of God for He is a good fellow and all will be well!

The true Christian fears God with a trembling reverence and yet he is not afraid of God at all. He draws nigh to God with full assurance of faith and victory and yet at the same time is trembling with holy awe and fear.

To fear and yet draw near—this is the attitude of faith and love and yet the holy contradiction classifies him as a fanatic, too!

Today, as in all the centuries, true Christians

are an enigma to the world, a thorn in the flesh of Adam, a puzzle to angels, the delight of God and a habitation of the Holy Spirit.

Our fellowship ought to take in all of the true children of God, regardless of who and where and what, if they are washed in the blood, born of the Spirit, walking with God the Father, begotten unto a living hope through the resurrection of Jesus Christ and rejoicing in the salvation to be revealed!

Where Will the "Experts" Be When Jesus Comes?

. . . and may result in praise, glory and
honor when Jesus Christ is revealed.
(1 Peter 1:7b)

Are you ready for the appearing of Jesus Christ or are you among those who are merely curious about His coming?

Let me warn you that many preachers and Bible teachers will answer to God some day for encouraging curious speculations about the return of Christ and failing to stress the necessity for "loving His appearing"!

The Bible does not approve of this modern curiosity that plays with the Scriptures and which seeks only to impress credulous and gullible audiences with the "amazing" prophetic knowledge possessed by the brother who is preaching or teaching!

I cannot think of even one lonely passage in

the New Testament which speaks of Christ's revelation, manifestation, appearing or coming that is not directly linked with moral conduct, faith and spiritual holiness.

The appearing of the Lord Jesus on this earth once more is not an event upon which we may curiously speculate—and when we do only that we sin. The prophetic teacher who engages in speculation to excite the curiosity of his hearers without providing them with a moral application is sinning even as he preaches.

Foolish formulas

There have been enough foolish formulas advanced about the return of Christ by those who were simply curious to cause many believers to give the matter no further thought or concern. But Peter said to expect "the appearing of Jesus Christ." Paul said there is a crown of righteousness laid up in glory for all those who love His appearing. John spoke of his hope of seeing Jesus and bluntly wrote: "Everyone who has this hope in him purifies himself, just as he is pure" (1 John 3:3).

Peter linked the testing of our faith with the coming of the Lord when he wrote:

> . . . though now for a little while you may have had to suffer grief in all kinds of trials. These have come so that your faith—of greater worth than gold, which perishes even though refined by fire—may be

proved genuine and may result in praise, glory and honor [at the appearing of Jesus Christ, KJV]. (1 Peter 1:6–7)

Think of the *appearing* of Christ for here is a word which embodies an idea—an idea of such importance to Christian theology and Christian living that we dare not allow it to pass unregarded.

This word occurs frequently in the King James version of the Bible in reference to Jesus, and has various forms—such as *appear*, *appeared*, *appearing*. The original word from which our English was translated has about seven different forms in the Greek.

Its prophetic use

But in this usage, we are concerned only with the word *appearing* in its prophetic use. Unquestionably, that is how Peter used it in this passage. Among those seven forms in the Greek there are three particular words which all told may have these meanings: "manifest; shine upon; show; become visible; a disclosure; a coming; a manifestation; a revelation."

I point this out because Peter also wrote that the Christians should "gird up the loins of their minds and be sober and hope to the end for the grace that is to be brought at the revelation of Jesus Christ" (1:13, KJV).

Some of you might like to ask the translators a question, but they are all dead! The question

might well be, "Why was the similar form of
the original word translated in one case as the
appearing and in the other as the *revelation* of
Jesus Christ?"

There may have been some very fine shade of
meaning which they felt must be expressed by
one word and not the other, but we may take it
as truth that the words are used interchangeab-
ly in the Bible.

Shouldn't have to try so hard

We do not have to belabor this point, and actually some people are in trouble in the Scriptures because they try too hard! The Lord never
expected us to have to try so hard and to push
on to the end of setting up a formula or a
doctrinal exposition on the shades of meaning
and forms of a single word.

Some of the cults do this. There are prophetic
cults whose entire prophetic idea and scheme
rest upon the words *appearing* or *revelation* or
manifestation or *disclosure*. Their leaders write
page after page and book after book upon the
difference between one shade of meaning and
another.

I can only say that I have learned this, having
been around for a while—if that cult is forced
to belabor a word in order to make a point,
check it off and give it no more thought!

If that cult that is obviously a cult with no
standing in the historic stream of Christianity
and no standing in the long corridor of ap-

proved Christian truth tries to build on one word's shade of meanings, you can just shrug it off.

Why do I say that?

Because the Bible is the easiest book in the world to understand—one of the easiest for the spiritual mind but one of the hardest for the carnal mind! I will pay no mind to those who find it necessary to strain at a shade of meaning in order to prove they are right, particularly when that position can be shown to be contrary to all the belief of Christians back to the days of the apostles.

So that is why I say it is easy to try too hard when we come to the reading and explanation of the Scriptures. You can actually try too hard at almost anything, including baseball.

A certain baseball team, for instance, at the opening of the season tries so hard to win that the players get up-tight, become jittery and jumpy, and they make many errors.

After they find out that they do not really have a chance at the championship, they become relaxed and suddenly they are playing very good baseball. They didn't change any of the men around; they just relaxed and quit pressing so hard!

I think this matter of pushing and trying too hard may also be of concern to the young preacher getting up before his first audience. His muscles tighten, his throat gets dry, he may not remember his main points—(and I have been there myself)—pushing like everything, trying too hard!

But we will never mature in the kingdom of God by pushing and pressing because the kingdom of God is not taken that way. Rather, you trust the Lord and watch Him do it!

The same thing is true concerning interpretation of the Bible. If we insist upon those fine shades of definitions, we may just be trying too hard and we may end up with the wrong point of view!

Perhaps we can illustrate it. Suppose a Chicago man visits his family in Des Moines and after getting back home, writes a number of letters in which he mentions the trip to Iowa.

In one letter he writes, "I visited Des Moines last week."

In the second, he writes, "I went to Des Moines last week," and in a third, "I motored to Des Moines last week." In still another, he mentions, "I saw my brother in Des Moines last week."

He seals all of the letters, mails them and thinks no more of it.

But what would happen if a group of interpreters were turned loose on those five letters after a thousand years, particularly if they were interpreters pushing too hard, insisting that there are no synonyms in the Bible and that the kingdom of God and kingdom of heaven are never used synonymously?

They would make their notes and insist that

the writer must have had something special in his mind when he wrote, "I went to Des Moines," and "I motored to Des Moines." Therefore, he must have made at least two trips or he would have said the same thing each time! And then, he must have had some reason for saying in one letter that he visited in Des Moines, which must mean that he stayed longer that time than when he merely saw his brother!

Actually, he was only there once, but in writing, he knew the English language well enough to be able to say it in four different ways.

So, when we come to Peter's use of this word *appearing*—just relax, for that is what it means! If a different form or word is used in another place and the same thing is being stated in a different way, it simply shows that the Holy Ghost has never been in a rut—even if interpreters are! The Spirit of God never has had to resort to cliches even though preachers often seem to specialize in them!

What it might mean

The appearing of Jesus Christ may mean His manifestation. It may mean a shining forth, a showing, a disclosure. Yes, it may mean His coming, the revelation of Jesus Christ!

The question that must actually be answered for most people is: "Where will this appearing or coming or disclosure or revelation take place?"

Those to whom Peter wrote concerning the appearing of Christ were Christian men and women on this earth. There is no way that this can possibly be spiritualized—the scene cannot be transferred to heaven.

Peter was writing to Christians on this earth, to the saints scattered abroad by trial and persecution. He was encouraging them to endure affliction and to trust God in their sufferings, so their faith may be found of more worth than gold at the appearing of Jesus Christ!

Common sense will tell us that this appearing could only be on the earth because he was writing to people on this earth. He was not writing to angels in any heavenly sphere. He was not saying it to Gabriel but to people living on this earth.

Now, Peter also spoke of this as an event to happen in the future, that is, the future from the time in which Peter wrote 19 centuries ago. Writing in the year 65 A.D., Peter placed the appearing of Christ some time in the future after 65 A.D.

We are sure, then, that Peter was not referring to the appearance of Jesus at the Jordan River when John baptized Him, for that had already taken place 30 years before.

Jesus had also appeared in Jerusalem, walking among the people, talking to the Pharisees and elders, the rabbis and the common people, but that had also taken place 30 years before. He had suddenly appeared in the temple, just when times were good and people were coming from everywhere with money to have it exchanged in order to buy cattle or doves for sacrifice. Using only a rope, He drove the cattle and the money changers from the temple. He appeared on the Mount of Transfiguration and after His resurrection appeared to the disciples. He had made many appearances. He was there in bodily manifestation, and He did things that could be identified. He was there as a man among men. But Peter said, "He is yet to appear" for the other appearances were all 30 years in the past.

Peter was saying: "I want you to get ready in order that the trial of your faith, your afflictions, your obedience, your cross-bearing may mean honor and glory at the appearing of Jesus Christ"—the appearing in the future!

No reputable testimony

There is not reputable testimony anywhere that Jesus Christ has appeared since the events when He appeared to put away sin through the sacrifice of Himself.

Actually we haven't found anyone that says Christ appeared to him in person, except some poor fanatic who usually dies later in the mental institution. Many new cults have arisen; men have walked through the streets saying, "I am Christ." The psychiatrists have written reams and reams of case histories of men who insisted that they were Jesus Christ.

But our Lord Jesus Christ has not yet appeared the second time, for if He had, it would have been consistent with the meaning of the word as it was commonly used in the New Testament. He would have to appear as He appeared in the temple, as He appeared by the Jordan or on the Mount of Transfiguration. It would have to be as He once appeared to His disciples after the resurrection—in visible, human manifestation, having dimension so He could be identified by the human eye and ear and touch.

If the word *appearing* is going to mean what it universally means, the appearing of Jesus Christ has to be very much the same as His appearing on the earth the first time, nearly 2,000 years ago.

When He came the first time, He walked among men. He took babies in His arms. He healed the sick and the afflicted and the lame. He blessed people, ate with them and walked among them, and the Scriptures tell us that when He appears again He will appear in the same manner. He will be a man again, though a glorified man! He will be a man who can be identified, the same Jesus as He went away.

We must also speak here of the testimonies of Christian saints through the years—of Christ being known to us in spiritual life and understanding and experience.

There is a certain sense in which everyone who has a pure heart "looks upon" God.

There are bound to be those who will say, "Jesus is so real to me that I have seen Him!"

I know what you mean and I thank God for it—that God has illuminated the eyes of your spiritual understanding—and you have seen Him in that sense. "Blessed are the pure in heart, for they shall see God."

The eyes of our heart

I believe that it is entirely possible for eyes of our faith, the understanding of our spirit, to be so illuminated that we can gaze upon our Lord—perhaps veiled, perhaps not as clearly as in that day to come, but the eyes of our heart see Him!

So, Christ does appear to people in that context. He appears when we pray and we can sense His presence. But that is not what Peter meant in respect to his second appearing upon the earth. Peter's language of that event calls for a shining forth, a revelation, a sudden coming, a visible appearance!

Peter meant the same kind of appearance that the newspapers noted in the appearance of the president of the United States in Chicago. He meant the same kind of appearance which the newspapers noted when the young sergeant appeared suddenly to the delight of his family after having been away for more than two years. There has not been any appearance of Jesus like that since He appeared to put away sins by the sacrifice of Himself!

We can sum this up and say that there is to be an appearance—in person, on earth, according to Peter—to believing persons later than Peter's time. That appearing has not yet occurred and Peter's words are still valid.

We may, therefore, expect Jesus Christ again to appear on earth to living persons as He first appeared.

My brethren, I believe that that is the gist of the Bible teaching on the second coming—we may expect an appearing! In Peter's day the Lord had not yet returned, but they were expecting Him. Peter said He would appear.

When our Lord had not yet come in the flesh, some were expecting Him. They said, "He will appear," for God had told the woman and the serpent, and Abraham and all the prophets, that Jesus Christ would appear to put away sin by the sacrifice of Himself!

Then one day He appeared!

He was not an apparition. He was not a ghost. It was not what some of the old madames with their spooky costumes would call a materialization. No one ever said that Jesus Christ would materialize, it was the prophecy that He would appear and that is quite different!

The Bible never talks about materialization. According to the promise of His return, Jesus Christ is not going to materialize, He is going to appear! You can throw out the word *materialize*; it is a weird word stolen and employed by the spiritists and devil cults. To materialize, a ghost today would have to put on fleshly garments and still walk among us tomorrow. To become material when you are not material, that is to materialize!

There continues to be a lot of curiosity about such matters, and I find that the curiosity that once killed the famous cat has hurt a lot of Christians. There is a certain "eeriness" about them—not spirituality. Eeriness! There are Christians who seem to be ghost-conscious and they can move right into the middle of a supernatural thing and feel right at home—right at home with the mediums, the funny wizards and telepathists and all the rest.

Personally, I don't feel at home with them at all. I cannot feel at home in the realm of the eery and the uncanny.

Peeping and muttering

The Bible calls it peeping and muttering. I do not accept the peepers and mutterers and I will never feel at home among them! I recognize, however, that there is a certain type of mentality that does, and when such a person gets converted, if he does not ask God to sanctify his mind, he will carry this thing right into the church!

In cases where this has happened, their theology consists of a lot of theological peeping and muttering.

Let me mention in this regard my dear old

grandmother, who did not know much about the Bible, but spent quite a bit of time with her dream book.

Her dream book was dog-eared and thumb-marked because Grandma would not drink her coffee in the morning until she had consulted the dream book to check up on her dreams.

I know there are people who do not dream very much, but Grandma was a dreamer. She must have had some dreams every night, because she would always open that book when she got up in the morning.

Her dream book had an alphabetical index, and for illustration, we will start at A for Apple. If she had dreamed about apples, the book would tell her what it signified. B for Beets, C for your Country, and so on down the line to Z for Zebra. She had a glossary that told her what she might expect on the basis of what she had dreamed.

May I comment to you that that is a dreadful way to live!

No wonder Grandma was a hustler, for she must have been miserable and worried most of the time, thinking about the meaning of her dreams and the results prophesied in that book!

Actually, Grandma was a sharp little woman and she taught me nearly everything I learned until I was about 15 years old. But this dream book thing was one of her eccentricities.

I don't know whether she got it out of a

similar book, but Grandma had a real thing in her mind about barking dogs.

More than once she told me that if a dog barked under our window, someone would die, sure enough!

At this point in my life I can only comment that if I had died every time a dog barked under my window, I would have been the best customer the undertakers of this country had ever seen! It seems that dogs delight in barking under my window and mosquitoes delight to come into my room, and if there is a fly in the parsonage it will head directly for me!

I have some kind of magnetic attraction for such things and if it had meant something in the realm of the peepers and mutterers, I would have been in a straitjacket and padded cell a long time ago.

I know these curious tenets do not mean a thing and I thank God for a simple, skeptical mind that has kept me from going through my time on earth worrying about such things.

Being of this disposition, I have my own feelings about the prophetic teacher who begins to unroll his chart to impress people with his ideas and theories! When he starts that, I begin to look for the exit because he is trying too hard.

Pushing too hard

He is pushing too hard, like the man who is trying to understand the Sistine Madonna by getting a microscope and examining the toe of the Virgin. You cannot understand or appreciate the beauty of the Sistine Madonna by examining a microscopic portion of it; you have got to get back and give it geography!

It is the same when you come to the Scriptures—you can be led into a blind alley by curiosity about some minor point of emphasis and fail to see the great, broad outlines of truth concerning the spiritual impact which the hope of His coming should have in our daily living!

The Word of God was never given just to make us curious about our Lord's return to earth, but to strengthen us in faith and spiritual holiness and moral conduct!

When Paul wrote to Timothy in his second letter, we find some of the dearest and most gracious words of the entire Bible:

> In the presence of God and of Christ Jesus, who will judge the living and the dead, and in view of his appearing and his kingdom, I give you this charge: Preach the Word; be prepared in season and out of season; correct, rebuke and encourage—with great patience and careful instruction. For the time will come when men will not put up with sound doctrine. (2 Timothy 4:1–3a)

Here the apostle cautions that our Lord Jesus Christ will judge the quick and the dead at His appearing, and then he links that appearing and judgment with the earnest exhortation that Timothy must preach the Word, being prepared in season and out of season.

A bit later, Paul writes more about events to happen when Jesus Christ appears.

He wrote:

> I have fought the good fight, I have finished the race, I have kept the faith. Now there is in store for me the crown of righteousness, which the Lord, the righteous judge, will award to me on that day—and not only to me, but also to all who have longed for his appearing. (2 Timothy 4:7–8)

Those who receive a crown

It is plainly stated, brethren: those who love the appearing of Jesus Christ are those who shall also receive a crown.

There are some who would like to open this up: "Doesn't it really mean anyone who believes in the pre-millennial position will receive the crown of righteousness?"

I say no! It means that those who are found loving the appearing of Jesus will receive the crown of righteousness! It is questionable to my mind whether some who hold a pre-millennial position and can argue for it can be included with those whose spirit of humility and consecration and hunger for God is quietly discernible in their love and expectation of the soon coming of their Savior!

I fear that we have gone to seed on this whole matter of His return. Why is it that such a small proportion of Christian ministers ever feel the necessity to preach a sermon on the truth of His second coming? Why should pastors depend in this matter upon those who travel around the country with their colored charts and their object lessons and their curious inter-pretations of Bible prophecy?

Should we not dare to believe what the Apostle John wrote, that "we shall be like him, for we shall see him as he is" (1 John 3:2)?

Beloved, we are the sons of God now, for our faith is in the Son of God, Jesus Christ! We believe in Him and we rest upon Him, and yet it doth not yet appear what we shall be; but we know that when He shall appear, when He shall be disclosed, we shall be like Him, for we shall see Him as He is!

Then, John says bluntly and clearly: "Everyone who has this hope in him purifies himself, just as he is pure" (3:3). Everybody! Everyone, he says! He singularizes it. Everyone that has this hope in him purifies himself as He is pure!

Those who are expecting the Lord Jesus Christ to come and who look for that coming moment by moment and who long for that coming will be busy purifying themselves. They will not be indulging in curious speculations—they will be in preparation, purifying themselves!

It may be helpful to use an illustration here.

A wedding is about to take place and the bride is getting dressed. Her mother is nervous and there are other relatives and helpers who are trying to make sure that the bride is dressed just right!

Why all this helpful interest and concern?

Well, the bride and those around her know that she is about to go out to meet her groom, and everything must be perfectly in order. She even walks cautiously so that nothing gets out of place in dress and veil. She is preparing, for she awaits in loving anticipation and expectation the meeting with this man at the altar.

Now John says, through the Holy Ghost, that he that has this hope in him purifies and prepares himself. How? Even as He is pure!

Dress worthy of the bridegroom

The bride wants to be dressed worthy of the bridegroom, and so it is with the groom, as well! Should not the church of Jesus Christ be dressed worthy of her bridegroom, even as He is dressed? Pure—even as He is pure?

We are assured that the appearing of Jesus Christ will take place. It will take place in His time. There are many who believe that it can take place soon—that there is not anything which must yet be done in this earth to make possible His coming.

It will be the greatest event in the history of the world, barring His first coming and the events of His death and resurrection.

We may well say that the next greatest event in the history of the world will be the appearing of Jesus Christ: "though you have not seen him, you love him; and even though you do not see him now, you believe in him and are filled with an inexpressible and glorious joy" (1 Peter 1:8).

The world will not know it, but he that has this hope in him will know it for he has purified himself even as Christ is pure!

Titles by A.W. Tozer available through your local Christian bookstore

Born after Midnight
The Christian Book of Mystical Verse
How to Be Filled with the Holy Spirit
Keys to the Deeper Life
Let My People Go (biography of R.A. Jaffray)
Of God and Men
The Pursuit of God
The Pursuit of God: A 31-Day Experience
The Pursuit of Man (formerly *The Divine Conquest*)
The Root of the Righteous
Wingspread (biography of A.B. Simpson)

Books of Sermons

Attributes of God
Attributes of God Journal
Best of A.W. Tozer I
Best of A.W. Tozer II
Christ the Eternal Son
The Counselor
Echoes from Eden
Faith Beyond Reason
I Call It Heresy
I Talk Back to the Devil
Jesus, Author of Our Faith
Jesus, Our Man in Glory

Jesus Is Victor
Men Who Met God
Paths to Power
Rut, Rot or Revival
Success and the Christian
The Tozer Pulpit (two-volume set)
Tragedy in the Church
Whatever Happened to Worship?
Who Put Jesus on the Cross?

Books of Editorials

God Tells the Man Who Cares
Man: the Dwelling Place of God
Next Chapter After the Last
The Price of Neglect
Set of the Sail
Size of the Soul
That Incredible Christian
This World: Playground or Battleground?
Warfare of the Spirit
We Travel an Appointed Way

Other

Gems from Tozer
Quotable Tozer I
Quotable Tozer II
Renewed Day by Day I
Renewed Day by Day II
The Pursuit of God Perpetual Calendar

For information on these and other titles by Christian Publications, contact us on the web at www.cpi-horizon.com.